Black

&

White

larry winget

Black & White

By
Larry Winget

Copyright © MMIV

Much of the information published herein has been
previously released in *thoughts and observations*™
and *more thoughts and observations*™.

Published by:

Win Publications!
A subsidiary of Win Seminars!, Inc.
Tulsa, Oklahoma • Paradise Valley, Arizona
www.larrywinget.com
800.749.4597

Printed in the United States of America.
Cover design and layout by Ad Graphics, Tulsa, OK

ISBN: 1-881342-35-2

10 9 8 7 6 5 4 3 2 1

Dedicated

to

ELVIS

Thangya. Thangyaveramuch.

"But what has a man, what has he got?
If not himself, then he has not.
To say the words he truly feels
And not the words of one who kneels.
The record shows I took the blows
and did it my way."

from *My Way* by Paul Anka
(best done by Elvis, of course)

Black and white. That's the way I view life. It's either right or wrong, good or bad. You are either on the way or in the way. It's hello or good-bye. I don't believe in gray. I think most people have way too much gray in their lives. They have compromised their values, beliefs and opinions so they can live comfortably in the middle, in the gray area, so as never to give offense. The gray is safe. You are never really called upon to stand up for much because you don't believe in much, at least not enough to really take a stand.

I admire people who take a stand. They don't even have to agree with me, though I always appreciate it when they do. I always take a stand. Too many stands for most people. I always have an opinion. Too many for most people. But you never have to wonder where I stand on any issue. I make it clear. I state it loudly. I am clearly for or against about everything. I like me that way.

This book contains lots of little black and white opinions about what I believe – some profound (at least in my opinion). And some mundane. Either way, you will know where I stand.

Try this: If it isn't personally hurting you – then mind your own business. If you don't like someone then just don't be around them – don't do business with them – don't hire them. But don't feel compelled to judge them based only on how they look.

If someone is doing something you don't approve of and it has no effect on your life, then what do you care? Leave them alone. They are choosing to live that way. You get to choose to live your way.

But don't discount that person's value. Some of the best things ever invented or created were done so by really weird subversive people – take Christianity. Gotcha.

Empty. All used up. My epitaph. That's what will be on my tombstone. It means that if you can eat it, I've eaten it. If you can drive it, I've driven it. If you can ride it, I've ridden it. If you can read it, I've read it. If you can listen to it, I've heard it. If you can say it, I've said it. If it can be done, I've done it. I don't want to die with things still left to do. And though that will happen, I want to spend the time I have doing everything I ever dreamed of doing.

Y ou can tell a lot about a person by the music they listen to. Ask someone their favorite artist. (Mine's Elvis.) Their favorite song. (Mine is "Unchained Melody.") Their top five artists. (Mine are Elvis, Van Morrison, Leon Russell, Merle Haggard, and Willie Nelson.) You can pretty much tell when they grew up, where they grew up, what kind of person they are and more all by the music they like best. I think that's interesting. By the way, a list of only five was too short for me. So I am going to add George Jones and Tom Jones (not brothers, by the way) into my top five list.

Smoking. If you choose to die that way I don't care. It is your God-given right and privilege. Just be courteous about it. And another thing, don't throw your cigarette butt on the ground. Unless you are really hardcore and smoke filterless cigarettes, then your butt will be there for a good long while before it breaks down or until someone picks it up.

Yes, I smoke cigars. I know the health risks. And I do it mostly in the privacy of my own home so as not to offend. Thanks for your concern.

My Philosophy of Life

Expect the best.
Be prepared for the worst.
Celebrate it all.

Life is short. Way too short and getting shorter every day it seems. So enjoy it. Become an absolute hedonist and just enjoy it. Stop being so self-righteous and pious and get your panties out of a wad and just kick back and enjoy it. No one really cares that much anyway. I promise. And if they do...screw 'em. What do you care what people think?? And who are they to judge you? So get on with your life and enjoy it – there's not much time left.

To all of you right-wing, evangelical fundamentalists who have turned over your brains to a preacher and the president and think that only your book, your view of God and your sexual orientation is ordained; to all of you West Coast nit-wit snoots who believe that it has to be Versace and walk down a red carpet to have any value; to all of you East Coast bluebloods who think you are superior simply because of your birthright; and to all of my favorites: the confederate flag waving, they-can-take-my-gun-from-me-when-they-pry-it-from-my-cold, dead fingers, mullet-headed rednecks; and to all of you who find yourself piously sitting somewhere in the middle…

It is time to stop thinking you are smarter than, better than, holier than or more right than anyone else.

Because like it or not, we are all in this together. And I mean all. With all caps…ALL. Not just Americans. Not just white people. Not just people who think like you, act like you, talk like you, have sex like you, believe like you, live where you do or are the same color as you. I mean ALL of us.

It is time to stop killing each other. Killing each other in the name of religion, justice, freedom, democracy or liberty. It has to stop. It is time to start taking care of each other. Feeding each other. Loving each other. Accepting each other. Learning from each other. And we all need to be living for that to happen.

Friends. You don't need too many. That's never been a real problem for me. I've never had very many. It's not easy being my friend. I am what you call "hard to get along with." So when someone is my friend, it's because they want to be. And I appreciate that. I love my friends. I will do what it takes to help them. Period. No judgment. No BS. No questions asked. I think that is what a friend is.

I don't ask much. If you make me a promise, keep it. If you give me your word, don't go back on it. If you say you are going to be there, be there – and be there when you said you would. If you mess up, admit it and accept the consequences. And if I am giving you money for a product or service, be at least a little grateful and smile at me some. That's all I ask.

Money. People say that money is over rated. No it isn't. Having money is a lot better than not having money. I like having it. I can do a lot of stuff with it that I could never do without it. So don't put money down. Don't joke about being broke. It isn't funny. Don't make fun of people who have it. As Reverend Ike says, "Make fun of the rich and you won't be one of us." Money is a good thing. You can't build hospitals, schools, churches, help the homeless, feed the hungry, or be charitable in any way without money. Earn as much of it as you can, give away as much of it as you can and spend as much of it as you can.

My last meal. Ever think about that? I do all the time. Not that I am on death row or anything but I still think about it a lot. So what would yours be? Mine would be chicken fried steak, mashed potatoes and gravy, fried okra, two fried eggs, fried apples, chocolate pie, iced tea and coffee. Can you tell where I am from?? And I know that it's all fried. Hey, it's my last meal so what do I care about cholesterol?

Kids. Most of their lives they are pretty much a pain in the butt. There. It's been said. They are dirty, messy and expensive. They keep you from doing what you would like to do so you can drive them to do what they want to do. And yet they are still about the coolest things on the planet. I love mine. I may not like yours, but I love mine. And you may not like mine, but I bet you love yours too. And do you know the most important thing I have learned about kids? They grow out of it. Write that down. That's my best piece of parenting advice. They grow out of it.

Want to make me really mad? Honk at me. That's all it takes. I hate to be honked at. When I am in the left hand turn lane and the light begins to change, just because I am not halfway through the intersection before the red fades and the green begins to glow does not mean that I am not paying attention. So don't honk at me. A guy did that not long ago and I put my car in park and got out and walked back to his car and politely asked what it was he wanted. I do things like that. People think I'm crazy. Then they leave me alone. I like that. But I don't like it when people honk at me.

Have you ever heard people say, "If I had a nickel for everytime I..."? The truth is if they really had a nickel for every time that thing happened, they would have about thirty-five cents.

Because of my beliefs I attend a lot of charity events. Because of my work I attend a lot of corporate banquets. They always have a band and people always dance. As a result I have formed this opinion: Perhaps the most disgusting thing to watch on the entire planet is a bunch of middle-aged white people dancing.

Fashionably late. Ever heard that term? Ever been fashionably late to a party or other function? Here's what I think: There is nothing fashionable about being late. Late is LATE. Late is rude. Late is a lack of consideration. Late is inexcusable. If I ever invite you to something and I say it starts at a certain time, then be there when I told you it started. Do NOT come late; it pisses me off.

Be quiet at the movies. Don't talk once the lights go down. I mean at all! You are not in your living room and you are not watching a video. You are surrounded by people who paid way too much to be there and we don't want to hear you or your comments. Don't chew too loud. Don't let your candy wrapper make noise. Don't dig around in the bottom of the popcorn box like a gerbil. And if someone politely asks you to be quiet, then be quiet. Otherwise I will call the manager and have your sorry butt thrown out. And please get there on time. You know what time the show started. It was in the paper. You looked it up so you could go to the movie in the first place. So get there on time so you don't have to stumble over me in the dark. And please don't leave your pager or cell phone on. Please.

larry winget

B etter to have a good divorce
than a bad marriage.

23

When I was forty I got my ear pierced. When I was fifty I pierced the other one. A little old to do that you might say. Yeah well, when you are forty or fifty I figure you are old enough to do what you damn well please. A lot of people don't like it. Tough. Some people won't even hire me because of it. I don't care. At some point, you should be able to look the way you want, dress the way you want and say what you want.

Gaseous emittances (farting.) Don't think that yours don't stink – they do. So don't think that we can't smell it. We can. And we know that you are the one who did it. And you might just be around someone like me when you do it, which means that someone will say something rude to you about you doing it and it will be said very loudly for all to hear in order to embarrass you.

My wife and I were at the movies when a huge woman in the aisle behind us decided she needed to go to the restroom. You can exit an aisle either by facing the screen, the more common practice, or by facing the people who are seated. She decided to use the latter way to exit meaning that her big butt hit the head of every single person in the row in front of her (my row). When she got to where I was, she paused to step around some packages on the floor and with her butt right between my wife and me when she did, she let a big one. The woman next to me said, "I wonder if she thought we wouldn't notice?"

By the way, there is nothing in the world funnier than a fart. It's a guy thing.

From a bus driver in Dublin, Ireland:

A guy discovers that his grandfather has died and immediately calls his grandmother to offer his condolences. His grandmother proceeds to tell him that he died while they were having sex. The man is amazed and exclaims, "But Grandma, you are 90 and he was 93!" She said, "I know, we were only able to do it once a week. We did it on Sunday mornings. He kept his rhythm by listening to the church bells down the street, you know, Dong - - - Dong - - - Dong - - - Dong, in fact, he would be alive today if it weren't for the ice cream truck."

Tattoos. They are addictive. If you get one you will want more too. I have several. I want more. I'm old enough to decide so don't give me your viewpoints or opinions. I don't live with you and you don't have to see me. My wife does, her opinion counts, not yours. The only suggestions I have about tattoos is to only get them in places that you can cover when dressed in long sleeves and long pants. And only get something that you are not going to be ashamed to show your mother. And don't put anyone's name on your body. Relationships are usually temporary but tattoos are forever.

Family. Who says that you have to get along with them? You didn't pick them. You were born with them. Now luckily I get along with all of mine – but that's just luck. Just because you are related to someone does not mean that you are going to be like them or enjoy their company. What about the old line, "Blood is thicker than water?" You are right. It is. But so is gravy.

Be yourself.

The motivational gurus love to say that. It could be dumb advice, though.

What if you're stupid?
What if you're an asshole?
What if you're a stupid asshole?

If that is the case, why don't you try being someone else?

Men are pigs. Men, don't argue with it. It's true. Stop kidding yourself. Stop trying to deny it. Instead accept it, learn to control it and live with it without being totally repulsive to the rest of the world.

Women. Live with it. It is what we are. Love us in spite of it. Forgive us for it.

If it were up to men, all women would wear leather miniskirts, thigh high stockings, spike heels and halter-tops.

If it were up to men, beer would come from a tap in the kitchen like water. Men think the best piece of furniture ever invented is the Lazy-boy recliner. In leather. Men are positive about the fact that the television remote control is the best invention of all time.

Men like lingerie. And whoever Victoria is, we love her Secret. She should be given an Oscar, an Emmy, a Tony, the Medal Of Freedom, a Purple Heart, the Nobel Peace Prize, a Pulitzer, the Congressional Medal Of Honor, and all the gold in Fort Knox. On the other hand, Laura Ashley is the Antichrist. See? We are pigs!

Men like cartoons.

On the other hand...men like to be asked how we feel and what we think. We like to be complimented on how we look and what we have on. We are sensitive. We cry. We hurt. We like clothes. Not all of us like sports. We may be pigs but a few of us are actually people – and most of us are pretty good guys.

So, oink at us every once in a while to make us feel good.

True happiness comes when you rise above the approval and acceptance of others and instead approve of and accept yourself.

I think everyone should be happy. I'm happy. I hope you are too. But don't rub my nose in your happiness, okay? Most of us are out there leading normal lives and the last thing we want is Little Miss (or Mister) Sunshine in our face telling us to have a superfantastic day. You know exactly the people I am talking about. Like those people who work for Disney. "Have a magical day!" I want to choke them. I stayed at one of the Disney hotels in Orlando a week or so ago and in the first thirty minutes after checking in I received four calls to my room from various hotel people welcoming me and wanting to find out if my check-in went okay and then to find out if my room was satisfactory and then from the manager a voice mail offering to do whatever it takes to make my stay a magical one. Here's an idea, if you want to make my stay more magical, quit calling me and put something other than Disney movies on Spectravision and put some scotch in my mini-bar. It's called a mini-BAR for a reason. Some would say that what they were doing is just good service. No, that isn't good service. It is annoying. Some people confuse good service with pestering people. You've experienced the overly helpful clerk; the one who hovers over you saying how good that would look on you and can I find your size and on and on and on. Wait. I could get really carried away on this one so I'll stop now. And have a magical day.

Avoid doctors who are fat, who smoke, who recommend drugs to lose weight, and who make you wait more than 30 minutes to see them.

Okay, if a place only has two sizes of drink – then they CAN'T be medium and large. One of them HAS to be a small. But try to order a small when they only have two sizes: medium and large. You can't do it. They will argue with you. "We only have medium and large." No. With only two sizes, ONE is small. You can ONLY have a medium when there are three sizes, not two. Medium means the one in the middle. And take that same logic to Starbuck's. Their small is a tall. Figure that one out.

Don't go to a church where the minister tells you that you are anything less than perfect. You are not a miserable worthless sinner. That is crap and it is not what God would say.

If a hotel is described as quaint that means it won't have Spectravision or a mini-bar. Room service, if they have it, will close at some ridiculously early hour. The furniture will be old. There won't be a place to plug your computer in unless you move the bed away from the wall. And many times, there won't even be a shower. How quaint. I'll take Caesar's Palace any time.

Toupees. Just don't. We can always tell. We can tell with the plugs and implants and all of the other fake hair stuff too. So I mean it; please, just don't.

Don't be noisy. Don't whistle, hum, sing to yourself, talk to yourself, talk to everyone around you, make obnoxious tapping, clicking, snapping noises, or pop your chewing gum. This goes double for when you are in closed areas like elevators, when standing in line behind someone, or when on an airplane.

Do not talk to someone else while you have me on the phone. That is rude. Do not take another call while you have me on the phone unless I give you my permission, which I won't. Do not eat while you are having a conversation on the telephone. And for heaven's sake, don't chew gum. I can hear it. And don't make me repeat myself. Pay attention. Take notes if you have to.

When I go out to dinner with a group of people, I think the right and easy thing to do when the check comes is to just divide it by the number of people there and to pay up. I hate it when someone says, "but I only had…" That bugs the crap out of me. Just be a big boy or girl and pay your part. In the long run it all evens out and you won't look like a cheapskate.

As a guy who spends almost every day of his life in an airport and on an airplane, let me assure you: your airports and airplanes are not safer. Sorry. All that the added security has done is piss people off. It hasn't made anyone safer. In fact, I think it is more dangerous to fly now than ever before. Now you have an airplane full of irate passengers who have just been subjected to having their underwear dragged out on a table for everyone to see just to find a pair of tweezers. I have seen them stand ninety-year-old ladies up out of their wheelchairs to frisk them. I have seen them tear apart a Barbie bag belonging to a six-year-old little girl looking for something dangerous. I have been searched so many times I have lost track. I have been told that it was an FAA regulation to turn on my computer. It is *not* an FAA regulation to turn it on. I have been told that my carry-on could not be carried on because it weighed more than twenty-two pounds and that was a strictly enforced FAA regulation as well. It is not an FAA regulation and no one has ever heard of it except for the one ticket agent at Air Canada that weighed only *my* carry-on. If carry-on bags over twenty-two pounds were not allowed you would have to pull about ninety percent of the carry-on bags off of every plane. Wait, I just figured it out. She was probably using the Canadian/American exchange rate: twenty-two pounds American would be about forty pounds Canadian and that's heavy! I have also been told that my cigar cutter was a weapon and that I couldn't take it on the plane even though I carried it on at least one hundred times since September 11 with no problem. I asked how it could be a weapon unless I decided to clip the end off of the pilot's nose, or got him to stick his finger in it or convinced him to hold still for an amateur bris. (This one got ugly – it was a forty-dollar cigar cutter – and they ended up keeping it.) I was even asked about the plungers I carry as speech props. When I told them that I made a living sticking them on my head, they told me they did not tolerate jokes. I told them that must make it hard to come to work every day then. They didn't get it. When you read about airplane rage, it is probably the airline that has caused it. Because it is an outRAGEously stupid process that is only getting worse. People should be searched, but let's use some common sense, consistency and brains. And let's make *that* an FAA regulation.

Las Vegas. I love it. It is loud, noisy, tacky, obnoxious, stays up all night, is stuffed with excellent food and is a little bit naughty. Vegas......it's ME!

I have decided to change my name to Random. Because at the airport, when they announce that there is going to be a random search it always means me.

When someone works for you pay them a good wage. Don't expect someone else to help you get rich while you keep them broke. And never mess with someone's money. Ever.

Never lie. My Dad always said he would rather have a thief than a liar working for him because at least you could watch a thief. Sometimes telling the truth is hard. And the consequences are hard. But they are never as hard as living with a lie.

Read. People just don't read. I have talked about this in nearly all my books. But no one read them so who remembers? What's really interesting is that book sales are up. New book stores are being built nearly every day. Know why? Good coffee. No one is reading the books – they buy them and they drink the coffee but few people actually take the time to read the books. I just read that people on the average read about 100 hours a year and watch television about 2000 hours a year. Almost 40 hours a week watching TV and less than 2 hours a week reading anything. Is it any wonder that people are so stupid?

Stupidity. I have no tolerance for it. There is no excuse. Education is free. Stupidity is a choice. You aren't stupid by accident. You have chosen not to pay attention and learn something. No slack for you.

The Truth hurts. That is how you know it's the truth. If someone says something really sweet to you, they are probably lying.

When I was a little boy growing up across from the Round-up Club in Muskogee, Oklahoma, and watching The Lone Ranger and Roy Rogers and John Wayne, I fell in love with cowboy boots. I wore them a lot as a little kid while pretending to be riding the plains. There has never been a time in my life when I didn't have a pair of cowboy boots. However, I rarely wore them. Somehow when you wear cowboy boots people think you are a cowboy. I'm not. That really isn't fair though. I wear tennis shoes and I don't play tennis. I wear running shoes and I don't run. I have even worn Bass Weejuns and I'm not a Bass or a Weejun. (What is a Weejun anyway?) But because I didn't want to be thought of as a cowboy I just didn't wear my boots much. But I don't care what anyone thinks anymore so I wear cowboy boots almost exclusively now. Wearing them somehow almost makes me feel like a little boy again watching The Lone Ranger. I now have around 75 pairs of boots. (I am prone to be a bit excessive. I used to have sixty-five pairs of eyeglasses.) And now when I wonder whether my boots are in style, I remember a quote by Raquel Welch: "Style is being yourself on purpose." Consequently I know, my boots are in style. "Hi-yo Silver…away!"

Perception is reality. That is so wrong yet I hear people say it all the time. Perception is NOT reality. Reality is reality. People used to believe that the world was flat. That was their perception. It was not reality. It was just their reality. Reality was that the world was round. Be careful when you hear that perception is reality because it might just be perception.

Cynicism. I get accused of being a cynic. Good. We need cynicism. If people would have had a little more cynicism then we would not have had the Branch Davidians, or the mass suicides surrounding Jim Jones, or all of the people being duped by Jim Bakker and his kind or the issues that the Catholics are facing with their priests right now. We MUST question everything. Religion, authority, politicians, the government, laws…everything. And yes, I did mean to include religion. God can handle the cynicism and the questioning; religion has the problem with it.

I love my dog. In fact, I love everyone's dog. I like people's dogs much more than I like them. (If you are a dog person, you will understand that statement.) Dogs always love you. They never judge you. You can do about anything and your dog will still worship you. Will your spouse or kids or friends or coworkers do that? Nope. Only your dog. Your cat won't. They hold grudges and get even. But not your dog. I love my dog. My current dog is named Butter. Butter the French Bulldog. Not the smartest dog in the world. A strong C student though. I've had Elvis, an English Bulldog. A struggling D student. Nixon, a German Shepherd, a brilliant A student. And yet, intelligence never really mattered much. Smart or stupid they only wanted to be petted and played with. And no matter how smart or stupid they were, they still drank out of the toilet.

The less people have to say, the
more they feel compelled to say it.

Discover your uniqueness and learn to exploit it in the service of others and you are guaranteed success, happiness and prosperity.

Without exception that is the smartest thing I ever said.

As I sit writing this I am in my hotel room in Maui. I am in Hawaii a lot. Nice place. The whale watching is a cool thing to do, and anyplace that has women in bikinis is fine by me. It just takes too long to get here. Which makes me wonder how it ended up as a state. Why did the United States have to travel this far to get another state? Why didn't we pick some place closer? Like Toronto? Don't get me wrong, it's a great place and I appreciate the Hawaiians and welcome their tax dollars and their votes and all that – but somehow if you've got to spend that many hours on a plane getting someplace, when you get there it ought to be a foreign country. You would appreciate the flight more, I think, if you ended up in a foreign country.

Black & White

I have discovered that very few places in this country know what barbeque is. First, it is not what you do on your grill in the backyard. It always bothers me when someone says that they are going to have a barbeque. You don't *have* a barbeque, you *eat* barbeque. In most instances it is a noun, not a verb. You are cooking out, or grilling, but you are not barbequeing (the verb) unless you are basting the meat over a bed of charcoal or some other type of fire in some sauce that is made up of brown sugar, tomatoes (ketch-up), a little vinegar and some spices. Second, in my opinion only Texans and Oklahomans know what barbeque really is. The people in Kansas City think that they have the market cornered on barbeque but I think they have missed the boat. Kansas barbeque has a sauce that is vinegar based and is very tangy. In Oklahoma and Texas, they have a tomato based sauce that is sweeter. I like it sweet. But at least the people in Kansas City have sauce. When you go to the Carolinas or that general area of the South, the barbeque is dry. What is that about? You don't even get messy eating it. So in my opinion, which has *never* been humble by any stretch of the imagination, if you want good barbeque, head for Oklahoma or Texas.

I am tired of helping people who need help. I have done it for years. One example of that is the help I have given beginning speakers who desperately needed to know how to become successful in the speaking business. No more. People who need help rarely appreciate the help or do anything with it. So I am going to quit helping those who need it. Instead I am going to only help people who want help. There is a big difference. People who *want* help appreciate it when you help them and usually will actually use the help. So if you need anything from me, don't bother calling. If you want something, then we'll talk.

My boys and I have always played a game based on the idea "what would you do for how much money." Stupid stuff like how much money would it take for you to eat a worm or to bite the head off of a rat and things like that. (My price is always much cheaper than theirs by the way; I know what it takes to make the big bucks and somehow a worm and a rat head don't seem like that big of a deal to me.) When my boys were about five and nine years old, we were taking our dogs, Elvis and Nixon for a walk. I had some dog biscuits in my pocket and I asked my son Tyler what he would take to eat a dog biscuit. He said he would eat one if I did. So I popped it in my mouth, chewed it up and swallowed it with a smile and then handed him his. He wouldn't do it. I explained to him the principle of "A deal is a deal." I wouldn't let him off the hook. We stood right there in the middle of the street for a good long while with him saying no because he didn't really mean it. I then explained the meaning of the saying, "don't let your mouth write a check that your butt can't cash." I told him that we would stand there all night if we had to but he was going to eat that dog biscuit. Finally, reluctantly, he did. Some would say that I am a harsh father. I think that was one of the best learning experiences of his life. As a man now, we look back at that event and laugh about it and he agrees. Most people never learn the lesson of "a deal is a deal" and daily write checks that their butt can't cash. I think they should have to eat a dog biscuit.

Are you afraid of dying? I am. I am not afraid of being dead. But that's a whole lot different than being afraid of dying. I just don't want to go through the experience of actually dying. Because regardless of how much you want to quietly go in your sleep, that rarely happens. Besides, that wouldn't really be my style anyway. That's what scares me. I don't like blood and guts especially when they are mine. And I don't like hospitals or being sick or disease or pain. See why I am afraid? I wish you could just skip the dying part and go straight to being dead.

Guymon, Oklahoma. Every state has one. You know the kind of place that when it's about seventy-five degrees everywhere else in the state, it is fifteen there? In Kansas, it's Goodland. In Arizona, it's Flagstaff. Flagstaff has mountains so they have an excuse. But it's always the same it seems. I watch the meteorologist come on and report that Phoenix is ninety-eight degrees and sure enough Flagstaff will be about twenty. Actually it is pretty stupid to even have a meteorologist in Arizona. They could actually just come out and say, "Okay, you remember today? Well, it's pretty much going to be exactly like that tomorrow." The weather doesn't change much. Except for Monsoon Season. When I heard about the dreaded Monsoon Season I had no idea what to expect. Then I lived through my first one. They should rename it the Cloudy Season. When your annual rainfall is seven inches it is ridiculous to use the word monsoon at all. Unless you live in Guymon.

Computers drive me crazy. I am a Mac guy. Supposedly the easiest computer on earth to use. And it is. I like my Mac. And it still drives me crazy. Does your computer drive you crazy? I think mine has a personality. And it hates me. And it beats me up about every other week. It decides to just stop doing all the stuff that it did just the day before. Why does it do that? And where is the stuff that I just saved? Where? And why is it that when I put a new program on, the old ones don't like it? Even right now, as I write this book and am trying to print it out, the computer is telling me that it can't find the printer. Why not? It's sitting right there not five feet away. It's in the same spot it was ten minutes ago when you used it to print so why can't you find it now? Did you forget?

About once a year mine gets so screwed up that I just put it in a box and buy a new one. Really I do. I used to call the tech help line. And after about a 3 hour wait on hold they got so frustrated with me that they would put me on hold to scream and conveniently cut me off, knowing that I wouldn't call back. I even tried a few times to hire a guy to come over to my house to fix my problems. They talked in a language that I just couldn't understand. So what does this mean? Nothing. But buy Apple stock. I am a great customer.

I can honestly say that I have no prejudice against race, color, religious affiliation or lack of, sexual orientation, or anything else that you can think of that you have no control over. Now regarding those things that you do have control over – that's another story. These are my big prejudices: stupid, lazy and rude. That's because you can fix any one of those. You are stupid, lazy or rude by choice. And God help you if you are all of those things. And I meant what I just said: God help you. Because I won't.

So if you have a tendency to be a prejudiced person, and you know if you are, then I suggest you change your prejudices from things that people can't control to things that people can control. Like your own prejudice. Maybe I could control mine against stupid, lazy and rude. Naah.

larry winget

Funerals. Funerals seem to be more for the living, and not the dead. I am going to be cremated and have my ashes put in an Elvis Jim Beam bottle. I already have the bottle. My family has even reluctantly agreed to it. But no one wants the bottle. You want it? You can have me. On your mantle. Just call my wife and arrange it.

Kids should be seen and not heard. You've heard that before. Actually a better statement is: Neighbors should be seen and not heard. That makes much more sense to me.

Did you ever notice that when someone says, "I only have one thing to say…" it isn't true? They always have much more than only one thing to say.

Don't ever say anything stupid like, "It can't get any worse than this." That is a challenge you do not want to issue to the Universe. Trust me, if there is one thing it can always get, it can get worse!

If you are unhappy, unsuccessful, sick or broke, please just keep it to yourself; the rest of us don't want or need to hear it. Don't feel compelled to share.

I walked into a meeting room where I was about to speak and the meeting planner said to me, "Are you going to make sure that we have a good time?" I told her no, I was going to make sure that I have a good time. Because if I am having a good time then others will most likely want to join me, but if I'm not having any fun, nobody is going to have any fun. I learned a long time ago that you cannot be responsible for anyone enjoying life except for yourself. It's not up to you to make anyone else happy. It's only up to you to make you happy. Will this work for everyone? It works for me.

I just started playing golf a few months ago. Actually, I am not sure that anyone just plays golf. It is like heroin...once you try it, it becomes an obsession; an addiction. It consumes you. It isn't fair.

I love it. The main reason I love it is because you never master it. No one does. Not Arnie, Jack, or even Tiger. So while I am now obsessed with it and I truly love the game, I suck. But I think it's more fun when you suck just a bit – it helps you keep your sense of humor about it. Kind of like life. In fact, golf is a lot like life.

There have been many books written about golf and the lessons we can learn from it about life. The best I have come across is *Golf For Enlightenment* by Deepak Chopra. I suggest that everyone who has ever picked up a club read this great little book. Good golf lessons and great life lessons.

I am not going to write a book about how golf and life are alike. Instead I will write a sentence:

Golf is like life: if you take it too seriously, you're screwed.

Sex is the coolest thing on the planet and our society has done its best to make it wrong and dirty. We try to legislate it. That doesn't work. We try to limit it. That doesn't work. We try to make it appear nasty so people won't want to do it so much. That doesn't work. In fact, that only makes people want to do it more. So what is the answer? More sex. There isn't one thing in this world wrong with it so just go ahead and give yourself permission to do it and to enjoy it. In fact: Do it whenever you can, wherever you can, and as much as you can until the day you die. And remember this about sex: If you ain't sweatin', you are doing something wrong. Now if this little observation offends you, it's probably because you aren't getting any.

Stress comes from knowing what is right and doing what is wrong. Everyone already knows the right thing to do. The problem is that we don't do it. We do the wrong thing. That is what causes the stress. Doing the wrong thing when we know what the right thing is. People go to stress management seminars. What a waste of time. Why would you want to learn to manage something you don't even want? So if you want to live a stress free life, just do what you know is right.

Women are like houses. They aren't really interesting until they get a few years on them. It is the wear and tear that gives them character and makes them more interesting. And the older ones, when fixed up with love and care are always the most beautiful, the most sought after and the most expensive. While the new ones are fun to look at and even fun to tour from time to time, and maybe even rent for a while, you really wouldn't want to live there.

Few people will turn to themselves to take responsibility for their results until they have exhausted all opportunities to blame someone else.

Learn to be selfish. I know that you have been told your whole life NOT to be selfish. But that is wrong. You should share your money and your stuff but learn to be selfish with yourself. Your first obligation is to yourself. You can't be any good for someone else unless you are first good to yourself. Take care of yourself. Then go share who you are with the world.

The most broken commandment of the Big Ten: Thou shalt not steal. You may say that you are not a thief but I bet you are. Any time you give less than your best, then you have stolen from your employer, your customers, your coworkers, the world and mostly from yourself. You must always give your very best. Good enough, isn't.

The stranger you are, the better you have to be. That's why I have to be really good.

You know what bugs me? Other than almost everything? A lousy handshake. One of those dead fish things that some people give you. Especially women. Women, who taught you that? Do you think that's feminine? It isn't. It's...just yuk. Grab the other person's hand and give it a good shake. Don't pump it, you will appear rural. And don't try to crush the other person's knuckles. Just make sure that the web between your thumb and forefinger touches the web between their thumb and forefinger and give one or two shakes with a firm grip. That's it. Not that hard to do yet it makes such a good first impression.

At the time of this writing, I am in my early 50's. I don't feel that old. I heard someone ask the question the other day, "How old would you be if you didn't know how old you were?" I like that question. How old would you be? I'd be 25. That's how old my attitude is and that's how old I feel inside. Thank God I'm not that stupid though. I've learned some things since then – not that I always do the smart thing – but at least I know better now. I saw an interview with Cher the other day and the interviewer asked her what was good about growing older. I loved her answer. She said, "Not a damn thing." I am tired of people who talk about how great getting old is. What's so great about it? My back hurts, I wake up groaning, my feet get tired and my hangovers last a lot longer than they used to. I'm smarter but it seems like there should be a better way to get smart without having to get old. I hope someone figures it out.

When in doubt, wear black.

Black & White

I recently watched again the movie "Ali" with Will Smith. I have always been a big fan of Ali and of boxing and I think the movie is well done. I also think Jamie Foxx did an outstanding job playing Bundini Brown. At one point in the movie Ali showed his amazement at the response he was getting after making some of his controversial statements, saying to Bundini, "Man, this is just unreal." And Bundini replied, "The more real you get the more unreal it's gonna get."

And that's my point. Very few people are ever willing to be real. Yet that is when life gets interesting. In my career when I quit giving the speech the meeting planner wanted and the company who hired me said they wanted, and just started being myself and giving the speech I wanted to give, my career went crazy – became unreal. All because I was willing to be real. I suggest this is a good idea for everyone and every business.

Who are you? If you know, then just be that. Unless you are a jerk. If you are a jerk, be someone else.

I have two boys. You have probably heard me talk about them in my speeches. Tyler, the older of the two, was a sniper/paratrooper in the 82nd Airborne in the United States Army stationed in Fort Bragg, North Carolina, and is now pursuing a career in law enforcement. Patrick was a fashion design major at the Fashion Institute of Design and Merchandising in Los Angeles, California, and now has his own business designing clothes. One is a trained killer and one is a fashion designer. Both pretty much the purest forms of my personality. My neck is red but my heart is lavender. Tyler does what he does because he likes to fight. Patrick does what he does because he likes tall, skinny women. So different yet they both came from me. How does that happen?

Funny thing about success: People want you to be successful – just not more successful than they are.

The Big Questions Of Life

Am I happy?
Am I healthy?
Am I serving?
Am I loving?
Am I learning?
Am I having fun?
Am I doing something I enjoy?
Am I prosperous?

If the answer to all of these questions is yes, then celebrate.

If the answer to any of these questions is no, then do something immediately to change things in your life.

When you go in a clothing store and see fifteen of the same item and know there are two hundred other stores in that chain and there are at least three other chains with that many more stores carrying the same item with at least that much inventory of that item, consider that a clue NOT to buy that item. It doesn't say it is in style as much as it says that it will soon be out of style.

I went to see Tom Jones in Vegas a while back. The man is in his mid-sixties and has three generations of women throwing their panties at him. I have never had even one generation of women do that. Hell, I've never even had one woman do that. I don't think that's fair. But he sounds better than ever and still looks pretty good too. Hope they still say that about me in fifteen years.

If your life sucks,
it is because you suck.

If your business sucks,
it is because as a business person you suck.

If your sales sucks,
it is because as a salesperson you suck.

If your employees suck,
it is because as a manager you suck.

If your customer service sucks,
it is because you deliver sucky customer service.

Some short lessons I have learned the hard way:

Never give yourself or anyone else a haircut after drinking three alcoholic beverages.

The essential words for a harmonious relationship... "I'm sorry" and "You're right."

When you make a mistake, make amends immediately. It's easier to eat crow while it's still warm.

Never pass up a chance to pee.

The two items no household should be without: WD-40 and duct tape. If it doesn't move and it should, use the WD-40. If it moves and it shouldn't, use the duct tape.

Sometimes you win and sometimes you lose. Don't be an asshole about it in either situation.

The best thing ever put on film has to be *Lonesome Dove*. The book by Larry Mc-Murtry was great but this is one time that the movie more than did the book justice. A story of friendship like none other. My favorite line is when Gus is lying on his death bed and he turns to Woodrow, his best friend for so many years and says, "By God, Woodrow, it's been a party ain't it?" I cry every time. And that's what I want my last words to my sweet wife Rose Mary to be, "It's been a party ain't it?"

Give up hope. Hope has never done you a bit of good. To me, hope says that you wish something would happen the way you want it to, but it could just as easily not. Kind of like shooting craps only the odds aren't as good. You don't need hope. You need faith. Faith says that you BELIEVE something will happen and you have no doubt about it. Hope is mixed with uncertainty. Faith is grounded in absolute certainty. Now which is more powerful? When you have hope, you also have doubt. When you have faith, there is no doubt. And who is willing to take action on something that could just as easily not come about as come about? Not me. And I don't think you would either. I believe it is much easier to take action on what you KNOW is true! It is easier to get up off your butt and do something when you are sure of the outcome. And when you have faith – that unshakable belief that what you know, you KNOW that you know, then it isn't hard at all to do what it takes to see your faith turn into something tangible. Give up hope and cling to belief and faith.

We all spend most of our lives trying to figure out how to get more. You get more by giving up more. That is the irony. You only get by giving up. You lose weight by giving up the stuff that isn't good for you to eat. You get rich by giving up the stuff that keeps you from getting rich. Things like too much television, lousy work habits, not reading, etc. You get more success by giving up the stuff that keeps you from being successful. That is how it works. Give up the stuff that is stopping you from getting what you want and you will get what you want.

What have you taught your children? I have taught mine what a good hamburger is and what great barbeque is. They both got that. Other than those two important things, they picked and chose the other things they wanted to learn from me. Tyler takes responsibility. When he messes up, he admits it. Patrick has discovered his uniqueness. He isn't afraid to be different and is completely confident in his individuality. I admire my boys. I have taught them important things. Just as they have taught me important things. Thanks guys, I love you both.

When you mess up, big deal. Just admit it, fix it and move on. Other than that, life is a party.

That's the smartest thing my son, Tyler Winget, ever said.

I never met anybody who didn't already know everything that it takes to be successful. We all already know. The problem is not that we don't know what to do. The problem is that we don't do what we know to do. The problem is not in the knowing – it is in the doing.

What I Believe.

Life is simple.

You can have anything you want.

You create your life: the good and the bad.

Love, service and giving must be the
motives of your life.

Money is easy and comes to you as the
result of serving others.

Service often comes disguised as work.

You can be healthy and don't have
to suffer sickness.

You live the life you choose to live.

You can change.

Words are powerful and shape the
circumstances of your life.

Thoughts are creative and control
your outcome.

Trust your feelings.

Whining and refusing to take responsibility kill your chances of success.

Results never lie.

Most people are lazy and need to get off
their butts and do something.

All good is rewarded.

Passion is a necessity for a happy life.

Guilt serves no purpose.

Worry is a waste of time and energy.

Personal satisfaction comes only when you
rise above the approval of others.

Everything in life gets better when you
get better and nothing gets better
until you get better.

When it comes to kids, remember:
they grow out of it.

God is the Presence of Good and the
Action of Love.

Love your work and by loving it
you will become excellent at it and
rewarded well for it.

It's wonderful to have lots of stuff,
but it takes more than stuff
to make you happy.

Fun should be a way of life, not something
you have from time to time.

Everything in life is a lesson. Refusing
to learn the lesson means that it will be
repeated until the lesson is learned.

In the long run, none of this really
matters much anyway so don't get
your panties in a wad.

Guilt is a total waste of time. So forget
guilt. It serves no purpose. You can't change
what has already been done. You certainly
can't change what is done by feeling bad
about it. Forgive yourself, learn from the
experience and decide to act differently
next time.

Concerning guilty pleasures:

Never feel guilty about anything that gives
you pleasure.

W e spend our lives going to work and making money in order to figure out how we can live. That's backwards. Instead, figure out how you would like to live and then figure out how to work in order to make that happen. Choose your lifestyle first. Don't let your lifestyle be the result of what's left over every month.

What do a fundamentalist and a lobotomy have in common?

They are both no-brainers.

We board airplanes all wrong. We let first class board and then kids and then we start at the back of the plane. No good. We should board first class last. It isn't first class to be on the plane and have people stepping over you and it is stupid for them to try to serve drinks to the first class people when everyone else is boarding. That just slows things down even more. So, board the last rows first – only put the window seats on, then the middle seats and then the aisle seats. And people with kids do NOT get to board early. That is a dumb idea. It does not speed things up. The only people who can get on early are the people in wheel chairs or who have other physical disabilities. Okay, so now the plane is loaded from the back to the front and from the windows, to the middle seats to the aisle seats. Now, it is time to board first class. Dear Airlines: this will work. Try it. You don't even have to give me credit.

Time management. Another dumb idea made up by people trying to sell seminars. Who cares about managing time? Instead we should learn to manage our priorities. When you know what is the most important thing to do and then do it, time takes care of itself. The problem is we have not clearly defined our priorities. We don't know what is the most important thing to do. In my opinion, taking care of customers is the most important thing in business. When you do that, everything else falls into place. In your personal life, it is being happy and enjoying who you are and what you do. When you do that, the rest of it falls into place as well. See how simple life really is?

What is the last thing a redneck says before he dies?

"Hey, y'all watch this!"

If you were in a Mexican jail, who would get you out? That is not a dumb question. Things happen. At least to me they do. Have you thought about it? I have. I know exactly who will be called. My son, Tyler would be there with guns blazing to bust me out. My friend and manager of my business, Vic Osteen, would organize the whole event, rounding up all the resources and coordinating the efforts of every one to assure that the break out would come off as planned. My A.S.S. (American Speakers Society) buddies would show up, get the jailers drunk, tell them jokes and baffle them with BS, while someone else actually did the work. And my Canadian buddy, Brad Campbell, would be in jail with me, so he would be of no use except to keep me company.

Who would get you out? My advice: Be prepared.

As you grow older you think more about God. I'm not sure why that is but it seems to be true for most folks. At least for me. When you are young you just believe what you are told. As you get older you begin to ask questions and look a little deeper in order to find out what you really believe. After a lot of research and personal searching, this is what I believe to be true of God.

God is not a he, a she or an it. God is the Presence of Good and the Action of Love.

God is not a personification but a unification. The unification of all that is good and all that is positive and all that is love.

God is not mean or vengeful.

God doesn't care who wins the Super Bowl.

God doesn't think you are special, but thinks that everyone and everything is perfect in every way just the way it is, therefore there is no need for the word special. None is above another.

God loves you and accepts you just the way you are; there is no need to change in order to have approval.

God is not loving. To say that God is loving implies that God can be something other than love. God can't. God IS love.

God doesn't need to punish you and won't. You punish yourself enough, so God doesn't need to. We are not punished *for* our sins. We are punished *by* our sins.

God does not judge. People judge. God accepts. You don't have to change for God to love you. However, you may have to change for people to love you.

God doesn't reward us based on our goodness. Goodness is the reward.

God has lots of things to say to you. But you usually have to get quiet to hear it. Your message from God is very private and very unique to you.

God believes in you.

God wants the best for you.

God wants you to be happy, successful, healthy and abundant in every way. It is not Godly to do without or to suffer. It is just the opposite. We are given incredible talents and abilities. Each and every one of us; no one is without these talents and abilities. They were given to us to use. Not to use them is a slap in the face to God.

God is more interested in you listening to God than in you talking to God. So many people are telling you to talk to God – and that is fine. I just believe that most of us talk way too much. It is more important to listen.

I speak at lots of banquets and luncheons
and this is what is normally served to eat:
something brown with white stuff on it or
something white with brown stuff on it.
That's all I know about it.

I ride in lots of cabs. I don't mind riding in cabs but I do have a couple of requests of cab drivers, not that many cab drivers are going to be reading this, but just in case you know a cab driver feel free to share these things with them.

1. If you drive a cab then help me with my luggage. Women should not take the job of a cab driver and then stand there with the trunk open waiting for me to pick up and load my own bag. If you take the job then do the whole job. (This is not a sexist comment, I don't care who drives my cab – I just want my bag loaded for me.)

2. Know where I am going. Especially if it is a major hotel. Don't rely on me to know the way.

3. If your air-conditioning or heater does not work then tell me *before* I get in and we have pulled away from the curb.

4. Have change. It isn't my job to get change from the bellman at the hotel or from the skycap at the airport.

5. Offer me a receipt. And give me an extra blank one.

6. Don't bore me with inane conversation. If I want to talk, then I will. If I don't then leave me alone.

7. Don't screw me. A clue is when the first question you ask me is, "Do you know the way?" Or "Have you ever been there before?" If I say no then the sucker gets taken for a ride. Don't do that. I am one of those guys who actually call and report it when I get screwed.

8. Don't smell. At all. Not good and not bad. I don't want to smell your sweat or your cologne or your cigarette smoke.

9. Clean your cab. I don't want to ride in a dirty cab. If it is dirty, it affects your tip.

10. Drive safely. I am not in that big of a hurry unless I tell you that I am. There is no reason for you to drive up the rear of the car in front of you. When I tell you not to, don't. If I tell you to slow down, do it. I am paying for the ride. If I don't like the ride, I won't pay for it.

11. Speak English. This is not a racist comment in any way. But if you are driving a cab in the United States, then you should be able to speak English. I don't care where you come from. I am glad that you are in this country and gainfully employed, that is more than many who were born here are doing so I applaud you. However, speak English. I promise you if I go to Abu Dhabi that I won't drive a cab until I can actually speak the local language.

Suggestion: Go to England. Look at the taxis. Take a couple of rides. That is how a taxicab system should work.

A magician was working on a cruise ship in the Caribbean. As the audience would be different each week, the magician allowed himself to do the same tricks over and over again. There was only one problem: the Captain's pet parrot saw the shows each week and eventually began to understand how the magician did every trick. Once he understood the tricks the parrot began yelling out in the middle of each show: "Look, it's not the same hat." "Look, he is hiding the flowers under table." "Hey, why are all the cards the Ace of Spades?" The magician was furious but couldn't do anything as it was the Captain's parrot. One day the ship had an accident and sank. The magician found himself floating on a piece of wood in the middle of the ocean with the parrot of course. They stared at each other with hate but did not utter a word to each other. This went on for a day and then another and then another. After a week, the parrot finally said, "Okay, I give up. Where's the boat?"

I like for things to make sense. They usually don't. Now that you can't take anything sharp on airplanes I am not able to take my pocket knife with me to cut open the boxes of books that we ship to my speaking engagements. So the other day I am on the airplane eating lunch. These days you don't get real knives to cut your food with, only those little plastic knives. But the plastic knife had a serrated edge and I knew I could use it to cut the tape on the boxes of books at the engagement when I got there so I stuck the plastic knife in my pocket. I had a connecting flight and as I was boarding I was once again searched whereupon they found the plastic knife. The poor things just went crazy because I had a knife and called their security supervisor over to talk to me. They explained that no knives were allowed on the plane. I explained that they had actually given me the knife on the plane. They said it didn't matter, that I couldn't take the knife on the plane. I told them that the flight I was about to get on was a meal flight and that they were going to give me another knife just like the one I already had on that plane so what difference did it make? They said no one was allowed to carry a knife aboard an airplane. That just doesn't make sense to me. Does it to you?

I'll try to be nicer,
if you'll try to be smarter.

Like that line?
Go to www.LarryWinget.com
to buy the T-shirt.

* * * * *

Blatant capitalism at work.

A few years ago I bought a Harley. I had never even been on a motorcycle in my life. But I had the attitude and the look and my partner, Vic, bought me a Harley t-shirt, so I had to get the bike. By the way, I agree with Jesse Ventura: a Harley is a bike, everything else is just a motorcycle. The interesting thing about riding a Harley is the camaraderie that goes on between Harley riders. First a Harley rider will always wave to another Harley rider. They don't know you, they just wave to prove the bond that exists between people who own Harleys. I think that's cool. And another thing: When you are at a place where guys who ride Harleys go, ummmmmm, let's see, that would be a biker bar I guess, you are always every other Harley rider's best friend. They don't care who you are or what you do, you are their friend. You can have a guy named Animal next to you covered from head to toe in tattoos and a doctor on the other side of you all acting like best friends. I think that is cool too. No judgment. No questions about who you are and how much money you make, just questions about your bike. The world should be more like a good biker bar.

So I'm doing a speech at some resort at a remote location in Tennessee. And I have to drive to get there. Now this is not my favorite thing to do. In fact, I wish all of my speeches were either in Las Vegas or at the Airport Hilton – someplace where I can just get off the plane, do the speech and move on. After a few hundred hotel rooms a year, no matter how special the hotel promises to be, it's just one more hotel room to me. But back to my story: I am driving along in the boonies of Tennessee and I keep passing these Yard Sale Ahead signs. I am not interested in actually going to the yard sale – I'm just noticing the signs. Finally, I see that the yard sale is right around the next bend in the road. As I round the bend I see three car doors propped up around a guy sitting in a lawn chair with a sign that says Yard Sale. That's the yard sale. Three car doors. Now that's funny. But not as funny as the guy who is also driving along past the yard sale looking at his car and saying to himself, "Hey, I could use me a car door." America. I love it.

How does the Gap get it and Neiman Marcus doesn't? How is it that you can teach a bunch of goofy minimum wage kids to greet customers and actually be helpful and you can't get a full-grown "sales professional" to acknowledge your presence, smile at you or say thank you?

The other day I was waiting to get on an airplane (pretty much how I spend most of my time) and the plane was typically late. This guy starts screaming and yelling at the poor gate agent (I don't usually speak so kindly of gate agents myself but this time they were truly innocent) about how poorly run the airline is, how stupid everyone there is, how ugly the airport is…you name it, this guy was screaming about it. Finally he screamed out, "This is communism!" I had kept my mouth shut as long as I could. I approached him, tapped him on the shoulder and explained that a plane being late was a lot of things but communism was not one of them. I then politely told him that he was being loud and making an idiot out of himself. He said, "Who the hell do you think you are?" I told him I was the guy who had just told him that he was an idiot. He said, "Oh." And walked away. I then gave the rest of my bag of M&M's to the gate agent and apologized for all of the idiots in the world.

Please don't be an idiot – I am running out of apologies.

Can't people read? Moving sidewalks in airports clearly say "Stand Right – Walk Left." Is that a hard concept to grasp? I am walking along following this guy on the moving sidewalk and he is saying "excuse me, excuse me, excuse me" to a group of loudmouthed, overweight ex-jocks (you know the type) who were standing all over the thing and when they finally let this guy through one of them said, "Who does he think he is?" As I walked right between them a second later I said, "He's the guy who thinks you are smart enough to read the signs. Forgive him, he was wrong." Someday someone is going to beat the crap out of me.

You earn slack. No one is going to cut you slack so stop asking for people to cut you some slack. Why should they? Life does not issue Get Out Of Jail Free cards for being stupid. Stop expecting the world to rescue you. The Lone Ranger is not coming. Clean up your own mess. Fix your own problem. Admit that you are an idiot and commit to do better next time. Stop fixing the blame and start fixing the problem.

I am not an economist. I know very little about the stock market. But my opinion about the economy is that there is nothing wrong with the economy. It is just as it has always been. Sometimes it is good and sometimes it isn't. Things go up and things go down. The only problem with the economy is people's attitude toward it.

We should show confidence in the economy and act as if things are good. If we think things are bad and act as though they are, things will indeed get bad. So get out there and spend some of your money. In fact, spend some with me. Then I'll go out and spend it somewhere else. I could use some new boots.

The President of a company I was hired to speak to called my office and insisted on talking to me. I rarely if ever do that. But somehow I agreed this time – I was standing right there anyway. He told me that he didn't want me to say anything about change. He said that he had promised his employees that change was over. I asked him if he really believed that. He said absolutely. I told him he was an idiot and that I couldn't speak to his group. He was a bit offended. Imagine that. But you know what? He really is an idiot. Now he is just an offended idiot. Change isn't a temporary condition. I wonder if he is still in business or whether he stopped being an idiot?

I am tired of people blaming movies, television, video games and music for the violence that goes on among children. It is a factor. But only a factor. What about lousy parenting? That is the real problem. If parents were involved in the lives of their children things would be different. Parents have left the parenting to the movies, TV, video games and music and then blame those things for the problem when it really is their own fault. You have to talk to your kids, play with them, take them places, let them know what you think is right and wrong, discipline them, tickle them, hug them, and even yell at them sometimes. Be a part of their lives. Know them. Know their friends. Don't blame others for the fact that your kids are a mess. If your kids are a mess, it is primarily because you are a lousy parent. There, I said it. Now deal with it.

I once heard Wayne Dyer say that there is a fine line between guru and asshole. I walk that line every day. In fact, I straddle the line most every day. One foot in both worlds. Sometimes I slip and fall one way or the other. You get to figure out when.

Is it rude to be truthful?

Some say yes. Those are usually people who don't like the truth.

The truth is not rude.

It is just the truth.

And the truth can't be argued with. It is what it is. You don't have to like it but that won't change it.

Some say I am rude. If that is the case then I am sincerely sorry. It is not my intent to ever be rude. I hate rudeness.

However, I love the truth.

"Truth is often uncomfortable. It is only comforting to those who do not wish to ignore it. Then, truth becomes not only comforting, but inspiring."

Conversations With God, Book 3
Neale Donald Walsch

larry winget

People come up to me a lot after I speak and say they want to be a speaker just like me. They have no idea what it takes to be a speaker just like me. Let me explain to you what it takes to be a speaker like me.

First, you have to have a lousy marriage and a horrible, painful, expensive divorce in order to gain perspective of what relationships are and aren't. You have to sell out to a major corporation for several years and let them own you heart, mind and soul in order to find out they don't really care about you at all, only the results you produce. Then you have to start your own business with no money, make every stupid mistake in the world, then do pretty well, then trust the wrong people only to end up going bankrupt and losing everything you have. You have to screw up in every major area of your life: relationships, finances, and business. You have to face your family knowing you have failed miserably and are so broke you can't even pay attention. You have to look your loving wife in the eyes and beg her to believe in your dream of being a speaker – something you know nothing about, while she goes to work every day to pay the bills. You have to tell your kids they can't

129

order a pizza tonight or rent a movie because
you are just too broke to pay for it. You have
to read a couple of thousand books and listen
to a couple of thousand hours worth of audio
recordings of other speakers and authors. You
have to humiliate yourself in the basement of
some church speaking for free to eleven sleepy
old men eating a cold salsbury steak lunch while
you are trying to figure out what to say and how
to say it in order to make a living saying it. You
have to put every dime you make for nearly ten
years back into the business in order to build a
real business. You have to withstand criticism
from your peers and other professionals in the
business because you don't fit the mold of what
they think a professional speaker should be. You
have to spend at least a couple of hundred days
on the road every year sleeping in lousy hotel
rooms and eating crappy room service food. You
have to be willing to miss your family so much
you lie in bed and cry because you haven't seen
them but about three days in the last month.
You have to spend nights sleeping in airports
because you missed your flight. You have to
drive all night long in a snow storm because you
know if you don't you will miss the speech and
you know if you miss the speech then you won't
get paid and if you don't get paid then no one

else is going to get paid. Then you finally make it and "suddenly" you are rich and famous.

Am I complaining? Not one bit. I have enjoyed most of it and I have learned from all of it. And I needed to go through every one of those things in order to be where I am today.

I only told you all of this to put in perspective for you what it takes to be a speaker "like me." So no one really wants to be a speaker just like me because they aren't willing to go through what I have been though. They just think I live a glamorous life and make a lot of money. While I do make a lot of money, a couple of hundred nights in hotel rooms a year is not a glamorous life. What they really want is the applause and the laughter they see me getting. I don't blame them, that's the fun stuff – that's the payoff. But they really don't want to be a speaker "just like me."

It is never as easy as it looks. Every successful person has a story – they have all paid a price – and that price is usually one you are not willing to pay. Know the whole story before you aspire to be like someone else or as successful as someone else and then and only then make your decision. And never criticize – you have no idea the price that has been paid.

"With my luck……"

Have you noticed that nothing good ever follows that statement? Why is that? Does everyone really have bad luck all of the time?

I am now at the age where my friends are beginning to die. And that age is not that old! It hurts. It hurts for lots of reasons. Sometimes it hurts not just because they are dead, but because some of them never really learned to live. It also hurts because it reminds me of my own shortcomings.

I had a great friend die recently from cancer. I sit here writing this saying "great friend" but sadly I had not kept in touch with him as I should. I moved – got busy – and just let the contact with him slip away. My intentions were always good, but I just didn't make the effort to call, write or visit. He didn't either. No malice. No problem. We both just let other things become more important.

I miss him. I should have told him how much I enjoyed eating hamburgers in his backyard and going to movies and laughing about our kids and dogs. I should have. But I didn't. I wish I could now. But I can't. It's too late. I messed up. I hate that.

So today I started re-contacting my old friends. Just to say hi and to tell them I love them. I am realistic. I know that I won't be close with many of them ever again. Too much time has passed and we are just in different places now. That's okay. I just want them to know I love them and that the time we spent together was special to me.

Life and death don't afford you many do-overs. Take advantage of the time you have so you live AND die with no regrets.

Feed the children. Feed the homeless. Save the whales. Save the rain forest. Mothers Against Drunk Driving. AIDS research. Jerry's kids. And on and on and on. Every one of these issues and all the others could all be solved if people would do something and not just talk about doing something.

You hear people say what a shame it is that we have children who are starving right here in America. You are right, it is. It is a shame to have anyone starving anywhere. Don't you agree? Sure you do. So how much have you given to bring an end to the problem? No really – how much? When?

When was the last time you actually sat down and put pen to check and gave a nice chunk of change to solve even one of the world's problems?

Most people talk about all the good that needs to be done and so few do anything about it. It's just talk. Talk doesn't fix much. I know. I sell talk. Money does.

I grew up a foot-washin' fundamentalist (thankfully I grew out of it). And one of the old time gospel songs I heard growing up was, "You're so Heavenly minded you're no earthly good." What a great thing for us all to remember. Our thoughts are so lofty – so full of love – so full of willingness to do anything to help. Anything but write a check.

Some do – I'll give you that. And if you are one of the ones who do, then I applaud you. But most don't. How can they explain that? Is it because they don't have enough to give? Hardly. Everyone has enough to give something. It is not because they haven't got it – it just comes down to they won't give it. But God will forgive them. God will. I won't. That's the difference between God and me.

Dennis Miller changed my life.

I heard an interview with him where he was talking about the change that happened in his career from being sort of a typical funny guy on Saturday Night Live, to when he gained stardom as a cynical, mouthy guy with an edge who rants about the things in life that irritate him. He said most comedians try to endear themselves to the audience. But he realized he really wasn't a very endearing guy. So he decided to just go with who he was and see what happened. What happened was that he got his own HBO series and became (for a while) a commentator for Monday Night Football.

Watching that interview reminded me I am not a very endearing guy either. And I was tired of selling out and doing the speech the audience said they wanted to hear and the meeting planners tried to tell me they wanted to hear. Instead I decided to just say what I wanted to say, have fun with the speech and do my career my way instead of the way I had been told to do it. I stopped being your standard motivational speaker and became The World's Only Irritational Speaker™ and The Pitbull Of Personal Development™. I stopped caring what everyone else thought and decided to be myself regardless of the consequences.

The result: Well, you're reading this book aren't you?

Thanks, Dennis.

Mr. Spock and I are going crazy. There is no logic in this world. I'm flying from Miami to Nassau on American Eagle. Several flights are boarding at the same time to various places and we are being loaded on various buses to be driven to the appropriate airplane. About forty of us pile on this little bus to go out to the airplane headed to Nassau. About that many load on the bus right behind us which is headed to Key West. After a few minutes of waiting, a guy comes on and tells us all to get off of the bus and get on the bus behind us while at the same time someone is telling all of them to get off of that bus and to get on our bus. They explain that we are on the wrong bus. Everyone bleats like sheep who only and always do what they are told to do, and they get off to switch buses. Everyone except me. I asked the guy why eighty people had to change buses when all you had to do was drive the bus to the right airplane. I explained that buses were mobile and could go just about any place you drove them – that is why they come equipped with steering wheels. He didn't have any answer except to say that we had to be on the *right* bus and the *other* bus was the right bus for Nassau.

It is no wonder I am bald.

Forget the Federal Air Marshal Program on airplanes. I don't think it's a deterrent to anything. Know why? You can't see them. If you can't see them, you assume they aren't there. What good is that?

Bars have big ugly burly bouncers who stand at the door for everyone to see. What if they just put the word out that there might possibly be someone in the bar who just might handle things if someone gets out of hand? Pretty stupid idea huh? Instead they put great big guys with no necks in black t-shirts two sizes too small with the word SECURITY on the front and back and stand them right up front to intimidate the hell out of you so you know from the moment you walk in that you are going to get thumped if you pull any crap in there.

That's how it ought to be done on airplanes too. The airlines ought to put great big uniformed guys with burr haircuts, bulging muscles, M-16s, clubs and stun guns with a name tag on their size fifty-two chest that says "Sgt. Badass" and have them stand at the front door of the plane from the moment they open the door and the first passenger steps on 'til the moment the last little old lady is wheeled off.

How is it that bars are smarter than airlines? Go figure.

I was riding on a plane one day flying out of Las Vegas and was seated next to a very old couple. She was at the window, he was in the middle and I had the aisle. I was writing on my laptop and had just typed the line, "A good divorce is better than a bad marriage." He was evidently reading over my shoulder and leaned over to say, "You got that right!" He then went on to say that he and his wife had been married for sixty-eight years. Isn't that amazing? I asked them their secret to being married for sixty-eight years. She jumped in and said, "I'll take this one." Then she added, "Just let the other person be who they are and put up with it." That may just be the best marriage counseling advice ever given. We have all of these ideas about how we want the other person to be. Chances are it just ain't gonna happen. (A fact which has bothered me a good number of times in my married life.) But people are who they are. Period. Put up with it.

I like country music. I can understand the words. I can sing along. I like lots of other music too. In fact, I like almost all kinds of music. I like good rock & roll, the blues, and because of my upbringing, I like southern gospel quartets. But all because I can understand the words. That's why I don't like rap music (an oxymoron for sure). I just can't understand the words – not that I would want to.

It has been said that music soothes the savage beast. Hoping that to be true, we play a lot of music at my house.

I'm at the car wash waiting for my car to come out of the wash to be dried off. Normally when the guys dry the car off, you give them a couple of bucks for drying it and cleaning the windows and the tires and all of that. So as I wait for my car I am watching two guys drying off and doing the tires and all of the extras to this absolutely deadly Mercedes 600S. When it's ready, they call out and the owner just goes out and gets in the car. He didn't tip the two guys a dime. There he is driving a $125,000 car and he won't give up two measly bucks to the guys who have just made it look gorgeous. I couldn't take it. I hate cheap. So I walked out and stood in front of his car and said, "Aren't you going to tip these guys? $125,000 car and you can't give them a tip??" He just gave me a dirty look and slammed his door so he wouldn't have to listen to me. I said, "That's okay, I'll get the tip for you since you're too cheap." Then I gave the guys five bucks. Probably the best five bucks I ever spent. Can you imagine how cheap he must have felt to have another guy pay his tip for him? And can you imagine what a good job they did on my car? Don't be cheap. The Universe always catches up with you and pays you back. And some loudmouth like me just might point it out.

In 1989 I listened to an audio tape by Earl Nightingale where he said reading five hundred books on any given subject would make you a world class expert on that subject. That appealed to me. So I went about reading as much as I could on the topic of success. Since that time I have read about 3,000 books on the topics of personal success, leadership, sales, customer service, relationships, religion, spirituality, team-building, finance, health as well as many great fiction books. Does that make me an expert? Probably. Does it mean I have mastered those things? Not by a long shot.

But there are a couple of things I am pretty sure of:

1) The number one cause of all personal failure is the refusal to take responsibility.
2) All human suffering would end if we would only love each other.

Why do airplanes have to be so cold? Are they planning to hang meat in there? If you get on an airplane and see someone sitting there wrapped in blankets from head to toe then feel assured it's me. I used to just sit on the plane and shiver because I didn't want to look like a wuss all wrapped up in blankets. I didn't think it was macho to admit that I was freezing. Then one day I was sitting on the plane and Mr. T came in and sat down right by me and wrapped himself in four blankets. He turned to me and said in that classic Mr. T voice, "It's cold on these airplanes!" I wanted him to say, "I pity the fool that doesn't have a blankie." But he didn't. He did however instill in me the courage to start covering myself up in order not to freeze to death. Bless him.

(Mr. T's real name is Laurence Turead. He was born on May 21, 1952, in Chicago, Illinois. And you thought you weren't going to learn anything from this book.)

A rule that is not enforced is not a rule – it is a suggestion.

If there is an exception to the rule, it is not a rule – it is just a good idea that applies most of the time.

Rules are made to be broken. And consequences are always associated. (Sometimes they're worth it.)

Jack Nicholson was right in *A Few Good Men*: "You can't handle the truth." People don't really want you to be truthful with them. They want to be lied to. They want someone to pat them on the head and help them blame the world for their plight. They want you to tell them they really don't look fat. They want you to tell them their stupid idea was really not stupid at all. They want to be told it couldn't possibly be their fault. They want to be lied to.

Trust me on this one. I know. I tell the truth and people don't like it. If it's your fault, I'll tell you it is. If you mess up, I'll tell you that you have to take responsibility. If you look fat or are being stupid, then count on me to make you face it. And people hate it. My family and a handful of friends put up with it. They don't much like it, but they put up with it. And my audiences put up with it because I'm funny and make them laugh, but mostly because they know that in an hour I'm history. But day in and day out people would much rather hear lies.

I think that's sad.

PS. If you like to be lied to – it's best you not hang around me.

Ladies.............. hats. Don't. Please. Trust me. Just don't.

Exceptions: Ponytails pulled through a baseball cap. Cowboy hats. But only real ones. Not those little fake ones that are shaped goofy or ones covered in fur. Only a real cowboy hat is acceptable and preferably on a real cowgirl.

I used to think the world would be a better place if everyone was just like me. In fact, I thought if I wrote enough books and gave enough speeches telling people to be like me, then I might eventually get at least a pretty good-sized group to be like me. Then it came to me: if everyone was just like me, who would I speak to? There would be no reason for me to speak. There would be no reason for me to write books. And more importantly, no one would buy them. I would have to do something else. Something that I wouldn't like doing. Either that or starve. So I have decided that I don't really want anyone to be like me. Then I'll still have a job.

The same thing applies to companies and their products. They advertise to get people to buy their stuff. What if everyone really did buy their stuff? What would happen then? They don't really want everyone to buy, just enough to turn a nice profit and stay in business so they can keep getting more people to buy.

We all exist to fill a need. When the need is filled, we no longer have a reason to exist.

It's a good thing there are lots of needs out there – otherwise, you might disappear. Think about it.

Hey guys, get that crap off of your belt. And I don't mean your name, Cowboy. I mean the cell phone and the pager and the PDA and the MP3 player (and possibly, but I hope not, the retractable key chain). You look like a nerd. No, you are a nerd. Unless you have the retractable key chain and in that case you are a janitor. I guess that some guys think the rest of us are impressed if we see they have all of that technology hanging on their belt. We aren't. The rest of us have that stuff too, but we use our pockets. These days if I can even see a guy's belt I am impressed – their belly is usually covering it up. So if you can show your belt, do so proudly. You are ahead of most guys. But whatever you do, don't hang all of that stuff on it. Unless you are a janitor with a retractable key chain.

Ever find yourself in a conversation with someone and they say something they think is important and then they follow it up with the phrase, "if you will?"

I won't.

Krispy Kreme donuts. Is there anything better? I did a speech with the guy who runs the company. I told him he was either an angel sent directly from Heaven or the Anti-Christ.

I was all right until recently because the closest one was still a long way from where I live. But now they have started selling them at my car wash. It is amazing how dirty my car seems to get. I'm leaning more toward the Anti-Christ idea.

W hile I am not really up to par on the history of American inventions, it seems to me the only things we ever really came up with are the athletic shoe and denim blue jeans. Thank you to whomever came up with what we used to call tennis shoes. (My first ones were J.C. Higgins because we couldn't afford Converse and besides, my Dad worked for Sears.) For blue jeans I guess the real thanks goes to Levi Strauss (again, thanks to Sears mine were Roebucks).

I recently shared this opinion with a guy who said how proud we should be of that – because our inventions were so useful to all society. He went on to say how much better that was than the French who had really only given us things that served no useful purpose – like art.

I told him that he was a typical self-absorbed American.

Art has more value than all of the athletic shoes and blue jeans in the world. (Though

I do think Heidi Klum in a pair of tight blue jeans should be considered a work of art.)

Americans seem to think we have all of the answers to all the world's problems. We don't. We don't even have the answers to our own problems. Otherwise we wouldn't have kids shooting each other in schools and children starving in the wealthiest country on earth. Maybe if we spent less money on the hottest new athletic shoes and the newest style of jeans we could spend a little on solving real problems. Now I don't think that not buying shoes and jeans is the answer, and that is not my point here. My point is that some people get so caught up in their perceived superiority – moral, financial, intellectual, spiritual and historical – that they forget other countries have been around a good bit longer than we have and don't have nearly as many problems.

That's my point.

Religion. I have a problem with it these days. Everyone has their own brand and believes that only their brand is the right one. A lot of them have their own book, thinking that only their book is the right one. Some even think that their interpretation of their book is the only right one. So who's right? None of them. No, wait. All of them? I'm confused. All of them make a little sense and none of them make complete sense. So here's what I've decided: the right religion is the one that causes you to love people more. The right religion for you is the one that makes you feel compelled to give money to take care of people who need help. (And that's NOT a preacher with a pompadour hairstyle. He doesn't need your help. Except with a new hairstyle.) The right religion causes you to give up prejudice and brings you inner peace. It causes you to care more about the world and all those who live in it. Anything other than that comes down to the brand. We should stop beating each other up with our brand and our book and instead focus on the true religion that goes beyond brand and book, which is simply to love each other.

I like a bargain as much as the next guy. And I don't mind trying to get a better deal. But there are some things you just shouldn't try to get a better deal on. One is on toilet paper. Cheap toilet paper is never a good idea. Think about it. No, better not.

The other is a tattoo. Don't be cheap when it comes to getting a tattoo. The last thing you want is a bargain tattoo. And you don't want to make your tattoo guy mad by trying to negotiate the price. When you hear your tattoo artist say, "Oops!" You know you are in trouble. Forever.

My son recently needed a part-time job to kill time and make a few bucks between his release from the Army and entering the police academy. He applied and was hired by one of those big home improvement companies that for the time being will go nameless. (I might want to work for them some day and while I am the way I am, I'm not totally stupid!)

At the end of the hiring process and while talking to the employment director, she said that new employee orientation would take place on the following Thursday and that he would need to call her to confirm that he would attend. Since it was Tuesday afternoon, and he knew his schedule (he didn't actually have much of a schedule to clear) he assured her that he would be attending orientation. She told him that she would not be able to take the confirmation until he *called* her on the telephone. She explained that their policy was that confirmation *must* be made over the phone by calling her. He told her that was silly as he was standing right in front of her and it was only a day and a half away – so just check his name off the list because he will be there. She told him no and handed him the phone number so he could call her later. He then pulled out his cellular telephone and dialed the number while standing right in front of her. She answered and he said, "This is Tyler Winget and I am calling to let you know that I will be attending orientation on Thursday." She thanked him for calling and checked his name off. He shook his head and walked out.

Stuff like this drives me crazy. Things need to make sense. Look at how you do business. Make sure that your policies and procedures don't get in the way of good sense.

Can you hear me now? Can you hear me now?

Yes, I can hear you. I can always hear you. You are eight people behind me in line talking on your cell phone and I can hear every word of your conversation. You are in your car six cars away from me at the stop light and I can still hear your music. You are sitting in the restaurant four tables away and I can hear your entire conversation loud and clear. You are at the movies three rows back and I hear all of your inane comments. (By the way, here's a news flash – the actors can't hear you so stop talking to them!) The fact is: I can always, always, always hear you. And I can hear your kids too! You are too loud. I am too loud. Americans are too loud. Go to Europe – people just aren't as loud. Conversations are private. People can still be heard, but only the person who is being spoken to can hear.

If I can hear you and you aren't talking to me then you are talking too loud.

And the American replied, "Huh?"

As you read these thoughts and observations you might be saying to yourself, "He doesn't like people very much." I LOVE people. I even like most people.

Collectively.

Individually, admittedly, I have some issues.

As a population, we humans do pretty well by most standards. The collective conscience of the world is making great strides to create peace, save the environment and feed the hungry. We aren't there yet, and we could do more, that's for sure, but we are doing better. As individuals, however, stupidity seems to reign supreme.

That's where my issues emerge.

America. I love it. And I am about as patriotic as I have ever been in my life. But loving my country does not make me blind to its faults. I think we should all point out its faults and the faults of our leaders as we see them. It is NOT un-American to do that. In fact, it is totally American to do so. America IS a protest. If it weren't then we would all be singing "God save the Queen" instead of "God Bless America."

When a restaurant brags about their home-made stuff – just ask them whose home it was made in.

I do.

Here is a word I hate: try.

Yoda, from Star Wars, was right. "There is no try. There is either do or not do."

When someone tells you they will try to come to your party, do you really expect them to show up? I doubt it.

When you tell someone you are going to try to go to their party, do you really plan on going? I don't think so.

Try is a word you use when you don't have the cajones to tell the truth. We should just be honest. "Are you going to come to my party?" "No. I don't want to. I would rather gouge my eyes out with a carrot stick than come to your stupid party." (Maybe I went too far. Go back to just "No, I don't want to." or "No, I have other plans.")

But it is easier to just say "I will try." Mostly it is an excuse to yourself. Try gives you a way out. "Yes, I will do it" is a commitment. And you can hold someone to a commitment – at least I do. You can't hold someone to a try because when they don't do it they can always just say, "But I tried."

My advice is to stop trying and stop saying you will try. Instead just give your commitment or don't. Period. Life would be so much easier.

By the way, I'm having a party soon. Please try to come.

The toughest thing you will ever do in your entire life is to go to the mirror, look yourself in the eye and say, "This is all my fault."

And it is. Good or bad, it is your own fault. Deal with it.

Ever notice how most people just let things slide? That bothers me. Nothing gets to slide with me.

Everything that happens or doesn't happen has consequences. I like to control my consequences. Therefore I have learned not to let things slide. It makes me hell to live with and work for but my results are important to me and I do what it takes to make sure I get what I want. So I don't take anything for granted. I watch the details that I personally control and watch the results of the people who work for me and with me to make sure they are watching the details they control as well. If the results are good then we are taking care of things. If the results are not good, then we are letting things slide.

Nothing is neutral. Everything moves you closer to the results you want or farther away from the results you want – every thought, every word, every action. I pay attention. And if you want better results, then you should too.

I recently got word I was not going to be invited to join a certain elite group of professionals because one of the members wanted the group to be more Christian and I wasn't quite Christian enough for her. Well boo-hoo.

First, I didn't even want to be a member and didn't ask to be.

Second, who is anyone to decide whether another person is a Christian or even better, Christian enough?

Besides, why would anyone think I am not? Is it because I drink? Or smoke cigars? Or cuss some? Is that it? What about a person's heart? Isn't that what makes someone Christian? And who gets to judge that? Not some human. And certainly not someone who is into being "more Christian" than another, that's for sure. And is the label "Christian" that big a deal? What about Buddhist? Isn't that just as meaningful? Or Jewish? How about that? Or Hindu?

Why does it matter so much that we label each other? Why are labels so important to people? Are the details really so important? What about results? What about motive?

I wanted to be turned down because I wasn't Taoist enough. Now that's something we could talk about!

Skin.

The more of it you have,
the less of it we need to see.

Rich makes up for
a whole lot of ugly.

M arcus Aurelius said that a man becomes what he thinks about all day long. In fact, many of the world's greatest philosophers have said something very similar. They were wrong. A man does NOT become what he thinks about all day long. If it were true, I would be Halle Berry.

My manager, Vic, once told someone, "Larry has no time for tact."

You think?

That's okay with me. One of my favorite quotes is this one by Harry S. Truman:

"I don't give them hell, I just tell the truth and they think it is hell."

(You know the little voice in your head that says everything you *really* feel? A friend of mine says I killed the little voice and now it all just comes out. May it Rest In Peace.)

If a movie is advertised as the "Feel Good Movie of the Year" then trust me – every guy is going to hate it. It will probably star Meryl Streep who will be doing some stupid accent and it will deal with heartbreak, death or suffering of some type. Or it will be a period movie where they all wear costumes from the nineteenth century and speak with a British accent. Or it will star Meg Ryan and will just be so cute you will want to puke. These movies will not make any guy feel good. So if you are a guy just buy your girlfriend or wife a ticket to that movie and then go to the theater next door and watch a movie with no redeeming social qualities and lots of gratuitous nudity and violence. Then meet afterward for some dinner and drinks and you will both feel good.

P.S. The dingo ate my baby. (That may be too hip for the room.)

Why spend time with people you don't enjoy? You do this, you know you do. You call these people friends but they aren't really your friends. So why do you spend time with them? There are plenty of people out there, about six billion, so surely you can find a handful of people you enjoy spending time with.

Do you enjoy your spouse, partner or significant other? If you don't then what are you doing about it? Have you tried? If you have honestly tried and it just isn't working, then move on. Dump 'em. Again, life is too short to spend it with someone you don't enjoy. If they don't make your heart soar, move on.

Am I suggesting divorce? Duh. Yes. It sure beats being unhappy. And don't give me the kids thing. No kid ought to have an unhappy relationship as a role model.

And if you aren't married there is no reason to even have a discussion about this, just move on.

Life is too short to spend it with people you don't enjoy.

Notice to all fast food employees in the world:

Stop talking to each other and start talking to the customer.

It ticks me off (and everyone else in line) to see and hear you laughing and griping and talking to each other behind the counter and then you finally glance my direction with a disinterested, "May I help you?" and then go right back to talking with your co-workers so you have to ask me twice what I ordered. Then you still get it wrong and aren't able to count my change back to me.

So stop talking to anyone except me – after I have my order and I'm gone then I don't care what you do. But while I am standing there, paying you to deliver a bare minimum of service, I expect your attention.

A fair exchange don't you think?

It's okay to have problems. Everyone has problems. Just don't wallow in them.

People love to wallow in their problems. There are support groups full of people who will wallow with you in your problems. People like to recant their problem, cry about it, hash it, rehash it (I hate hash), talk about it, think about it, analyze it, become introspective of it, meditate on it, write about it, journal it . . . everything but fix it and get past it!

So you messed up. Who hasn't? Name one person. Everyone has. And will continue to. So move on!

Am I trashing support groups? Have I been unclear here? Yes! I am. Because I have yet to see one that says, "Yes, you messed up . . . big deal! Admit it, take responsibility for it, say you are sorry, fix it, get over it, move on to the next thing!" Now if you are a part of a support group that is like that, then accept my apology. However, if you are part of one where everyone gets together and wallows in the misery of each other's problems, then get the hell out of that group now! Dump the whining losers and find yourself some real friends.

You can circle up, hold hands and sing Kum Ba Yah for the rest of your life and until you shake it off and get started with the process of creating a new life you are going to remain miserable. And you deserve to.

Don't bother telling me how successful you are. First, I don't care. Second, I won't be impressed. Third, if you have to tell me, I'll think you are lying.

As I write this I am sitting on an airplane next to a guy who has just spent the last fifteen minutes trying to convince me how rich, successful and important he is. (If you know anything about me at all then you know much I hate to "chat" with people on airplanes.) As he droned on and on about billion dollar this and VP of that and huge sales force this and international office that, all I could focus on was the worn through sock sticking out of the scuffed up shoe with the hole in the sole.

I know that success doesn't always show – but it *usually* does.

At the same time there is a guy across the aisle from me in a pair of ragged jeans, beat up sandals and a shirt that I wouldn't wear to a goat breeding. He is successful. You can just tell. You can almost always tell.

Success is not always about the clothes you wear, or the jewelry on your hands and wrist or the thickness of your wad of cash. But it still shows whether these things are evident or not. People of very nominal means sometimes have it and some rich people don't. It is a presence you give off. Success has an aura – a feeling.

The more you try to force that feeling, the more you try to shove it down someone's throat, the more you end up just looking sad. (I know a guy who carries around his income tax return to prove he is a millionaire. Really!)

Relax. If you are successful it will show. You won't have to prove it.

Just go out there and give it **110%**!! Yep, that's what will make you successful. No? Well the motivational gurus are sure that will do it. I've heard them say so.

Let me help you with this.

You can't give **110%**. It is impossible. **100%** is all there is. **100%** is MAXIMUM. There isn't **110%** – it doesn't exist and you can't give it.

I'll give you this: you can give more than you think you can. You always have more to give. But you can't give more than there is. The best you can do is **100%**.

It is like getting on the airplane and having the flight attendant announce that the flight is going to be extremely full. No it isn't. The flight can only be full. Full is **100%**. It can't be extremely full – it can only be full.

We are so prone to exaggeration. I don't mind that, usually. I make my living exaggerating a bit. But I don't like exaggeration when it comes to matters of practicality.

So go get on that full airplane and give it **100%**. I don't know what good it will do you but at least you will be more accurate.

Don't be late. There is never an excuse. Car accident on the highway? You should have allowed time for that. You had a flat? Again, should have allowed time. Last appointment ran long? Call me to let me know you are running behind.

Being late is disrespectful – plain and simple. It says that you don't respect my time enough to bother making the effort to be on time.

Here's what I think is fair. If I hire you to meet me at my house to work on something and you promise to be there at 10:00 AM and then you don't show until 11:00, then I get to either dock your bill by your hourly rate for making me wait on you or I get to charge you my hourly rate for having to wait. (Trust me – you don't want to pay my hourly rate!)

Doesn't that sound fair? If all of us instituted that practice then people would start to be on time.

When I hire a plumber or electrician on the telephone, that's what I tell them we are going to do. I tell them I won't tolerate them being late and if they can't meet their commitment to just tell me now and I'll be happy to call someone who is able to keep their word. A lot of people just won't work with me. That's okay. I don't care. There are long lists of plumbers in the book – there will be one who will honor his commitment. But isn't it interesting they see me as the bad guy simply because once they set the appointment, I expect them to keep it?

Now that's just sad. No, it's pitiful.

You have figured out by now how I feel about stupidity. And while some think me rude I feel you may be judging me unfairly. Not that I care too much about that but I think you should understand a bit more about my feelings on the subject.

There is a major difference between stupidity and ignorance. Stupidity is when you know what to do but won't do it. Ignorance doesn't even know. Ignorance doesn't have a clue.

Jesus said, "Forgive them for they know not what they do." Ignorance is forgivable. But not for long. You don't get to be ignorant forever. After a while you should have a clue. But remember as soon as you have a clue, then you are responsible for doing something with it. If you don't, then you're stupid.

Why do people who are not successful think they have the right to argue with those who are successful about what it takes to be successful? They obviously don't know what they are talking about or they would be successful. Instead they should shut up and listen and try to learn something. But no, they want to argue.

Speakers call or write me and ask me to help them become successful. Then when I tell them what to do they want to argue with me. They ask me to defend my position. I don't have to defend my position – it works – that's why you called me, remember? And if you aren't successful, then you don't even have a position to defend. So stop arguing!

People wonder why after a while, successful people cut themselves off from others. It is because they get tired of having to defend their position of what works. Me, I didn't cut myself off, I just started charging for the help. It's not that I need the money from helping people (though I never turn down money). It's that when someone pays for something they ask better questions, they take better notes and they feel obligated to do something with the information. And best of all, they don't argue with me.

I used to go to a church (a major Protestant denomination) that every week had the congregation stand and recite together their confession "of sorts."

There is a line in this confession that says "behold our manifold wickedness." What a stupid thing to say. Why would you want to proclaim that about yourself? I never really felt particularly "manifoldly wicked." I always thought I was pretty good – not perfect – but not too bad either. So it bothered me to stand and proclaim to God and all the others in the church and mostly to myself that I was "manifoldly wicked."

So I quit going to that church. A simple solution. (Except when a few asked why I quit going and I told them I was not "manifoldly wicked" and was tired of saying I was. That is when it got complicated.)

I come from the school of thought that says what you say about yourself has a tendency to come true. And because I didn't want to become manifoldly wicked I quit saying stuff like that.

That's one of the problems I have with the twelve step programs. To me it doesn't make sense to stand and have the first thing out of your mouth be: "I am an alcoholic." I know those programs help lots of people but I still think a more powerful statement is: "I am sober."

Say what you want to be true about yourself. Proclaim to God and to the world and to yourself the kind of person you want to be. Then you have a better shot at becoming that person instead of reminding yourself of everything you don't want to be.

Give a guy a uniform, a badge and a gun
and suddenly he is the biggest baddest
meanest mother that ever walked. I am
NOT talking about people in the military
or people in law enforcement. I am talking
about airport security, hotel security, movie
security and best of all: mall cops. Ever see
the movie about security guards, *Armed
and Dangerous,* with Eugene Levy and John
Candy? Sadly it seems a bit too accurate to
me. Do these guys really think they could
shoot someone and hit them? Or outrun
anyone other than the little old blue-haired
lady with the walker? Yet they think they are
Buford Pusser. I have no problem with them
being employed – good for them. I only have
a problem with their inflated egos and the
seriousness with which they take themselves.
Calm down, Barney Fife.

larry winget

Take your job seriously,
not yourself.

Someone asked me recently what I loved most about my wife.

Good question. Easy answer for me.

What I love most about Rose Mary is that she loves me.

Believe it or not, that is not an easy thing to do.

I am just almost impossible. I am loud. Obnoxious. Intolerant. Demanding. A perfectionist. Impatient. And those are my good traits.

But Rose Mary loves me. Regardless. (Or for the illiterate: irregardless.)

That's what I love most about her: she just loves me. Somehow she sees the good things in me and forgives me for the other things.

What could be better than that?

This is a sad day. Today, my son realized that Dad has been right all along and people really are stupid.

My son is a typical college student. He is broke. Weren't you? (If you weren't then keep it to yourself because those of us who lived on Mac & Cheese at four boxes for a dollar don't want to hear it.) So since he is broke he watches his pennies pretty closely. And he is VERY conscientious. He knows the value of having good credit so he always pays his bills on time.

Warning: the rest of this rant contains real names. They have not been changed to protect the innocent – there are none.

So he called AT&T (yep, I actually named them) today to pay his cell phone bill with his checking account debit card. Letitia (her real name), took the information and then said, "Oops, I have charged you twice." He said, that's okay just credit one of the charges back. She explained that she couldn't do that – that it had to be reviewed and would take seven to ten business days to go back into his account. He asked for a supervisor. (I have trained him well – everyone has a boss.) The supervisor said seven to ten days. He asked for her supervisor. Seven to ten business days. He explained that left him with NO money. Nada – none – nothing. They said they were sorry but that is how the system works. He was incredulous. Yep, his word – he's a smart kid. He said, "Your employee makes the mistake and now I am left with no money for ten business days? Why should I be broke because your employee makes a mistake?" Seven to ten days is their only answer. So he calls his bank (Wells Fargo) to warn them he has checks out and explains what has happened. They are sorry and agree not to send his checks back nor to charge an overdraft charge. (Some people are nice some of the time.)

Then he called me. He wondered if they were treating him like that just because he was a kid. I told him bad service was not age discriminatory.

But it's a tough day when you learn these horrible lessons:

People are stupid.

No one really cares about you or your problems.

Customer service is a joke.

P.S. There are exceptions. Please help me find them.

P.S.S. He called them back in ten business days and they claimed no payments had been made at all on his account and they were going to turn him over to collections. He went crazy but he had them. He had his bank statement with all the dates and deductions. Three people later they admitted they had switched computer systems and some people's payments had been lost.

Again, there are no innocents.

Consistency is definitely one of the keys to success. And the interesting thing is that you don't have to be consistently good. You just have to be consistent. For instance: look at McDonald's. A Big Mac is the same no matter where you get it. I have had one in Paris (yep, I did it – I'm not proud of it but I was just getting off the plane and was starving.) I have had one in Tijuana (yep, I did it and this time, I am proud of it.) And I have had one in Muskogee, Oklahoma, and New York City and most other major cities as well as many airports. And the point is not whether the burger is good or bad – the point is that you can count on it being the same every time. You are glad it is the same – good or bad. You can count on it. And sometimes you are willing to accept bad if you can count on it – you may choose bad out of convenience or speed or price. But it is the SAME – and that's good. You want sameness in some things.

Like at airport security. I want the rules to be the same at all airports. I want to be able to count on the same procedures every time. Either my computer comes out and gets turned on or it doesn't. Either my shoes have to come off or they don't. I don't care what they do – I just want it to be the same every time.

Same goes for the bank and the mall and with almost any store policy – policies are *not* open for individual interpretation. They are policies that are probably written down and if you are going to have them at all they should be followed every time regardless of employee or situation or customer.

Let me make it clear: I don't have to like your policies. I don't have to agree with them. But I want to be able to count on them being the same every time, in every situation, for everyone. And the nice thing is if I don't like your policy (Radio Shack) then I don't have to shop there.

Air quotes. You know what I mean. When you make those little squinchy things with the first two fingers on both hands that you think look like quotation marks – and you do it to emphasize a word or phrase you are saying that you think is important. Got the picture? Don't do it. You look like an idiot.

About the worst thing you can do is believe your own publicity.

Every special interest group seems to be their own worst enemy.

Examples: National Organization of Women. Have you ever seen these women? Do you really believe they represent all, or even most, women nationally? Not me. The leaders for that group I see speaking look more like Bulgarian shot-putters than the women I see in the workplace. How about "The Religious Right?" (Not that I think they are anywhere close to "right.") Some of those people are good folks who are only conservative in their beliefs. That's fine with me – no problem. But then they prance out Jerry Falwell and Pat Robertson and they all just look stupid. Now these are only two examples – because the same applies to almost any group. Every organization has a radical extremist faction. In fact, in my organization I am the radical extremist faction. (Bet that surprises you, doesn't it?)

I think it is fine to have extremists – but I think we have to be careful when we judge the whole organization by one faction.

The few crazies in any organization give the whole organization a bad name which does much more harm than good. They try to bring attention to their cause and get sympathy or money or whatever and only end up making most of us disgusted with the cause.

Whose fault is it? Our own. The goofy, loud-mouthed militants in any organization get the media coverage because they are goofy, loudmouthed and militant – it's good TV. We watch it because we are voyeuristic puppets who want more and more outrageous stuff on television. So the media covers it and the groups become more and more crazy in order to get the attention. A vicious circle for sure.

We had some friends over for dinner last week. At the end of the evening, my friend said to me, "Did you realize that most of your conversations and stories revolve around the word "today?" It is the predominant word in your vocabulary."

It caused me to think. He is right. My wife agreed and so did my kids.

If something is a good idea – why wait? I am not much of a planner. I am a doer. And I want it done now. Not tomorrow. I may be dead tomorrow. I want it done today.

And I am impatient. An idea needs energy to become reality. And energy fades when not acted upon. So I act immediately in order to give my idea more energy.

General Patton said, "A good plan violently implemented today is better than a perfect plan perfectly implemented tomorrow." (paraphrased by Larry)

What are you waiting for?

For more money? Better weather? Different conditions? What?

Just do it. Period. Get off your butt and do it. Stop waiting. The time is now.

Okay, you are at the drive-in bank. You pull up to the window because it is finally your turn and you *suddenly* realize that your deposit slip is not made out.

Are you kidding me?

You didn't know before then? What have you been doing for the last ten minutes – looking at the bumper of the car in front of you and watching everyone else hand over their deposit slip?

Next time.........think!!

Or deal with the guy behind you – and sorry, it may be me.

Get a clue. Really. That's all I am going to say about it. Just get a clue.

(If you have no idea what I am talking about here – you don't have a clue.)

I just read in the paper about a guy who sends money to people to help them with their bills. Just a couple of hundred here and there to help them through bad times. I think this is bad judgment. I applaud his heart but have a problem with his method. I think we should help people but I don't really think he is helping people. It goes back to the ancient saying: "Give a man a fish and feed him for a day. Teach a man to fish and feed him for a lifetime." (Or something like that.)

This man with the good motive is only giving these people a fish. Next month or the month after, I believe they will be right back in the same predicament. Therefore, I don't think he really helped them much.

Yes, he is a good man. He has a good heart. What he did was a real act of kindness. However, I think he should have sent them a book. Or paid their way to a seminar. Or shown them how to spend wisely or save some money or how to invest their money. I think we help people most when we give them the information to do better forever.

Yes, some people have an immediate need that needs attention. But after the need is met and the attention given, have they learned not to get in the same trouble again? I think sometimes we don't help by easing their pain with our generosity. I think sometimes the pain is the best teacher.

Another ancient saying says: "Adversity introduces a man to himself." More people should look in the mirror and say hello for what may be the first time. And after they meet themselves, they should get off their butts and get smarter, and work harder and help themselves out of their mess. Then a lesson has been learned. Then real change has taken place.

Help is different than a handout. Help people more. But give fewer handouts.

I have been accused of being a know-it-all. Imagine that. However, I want to make it clear I do not know it all. And I even know that I don't know it all which will come as a surprise to some. In fact, the more I learn, the more I realize I don't really know all that much. However, while I understand that in the grand scheme of things I know very little, I am still quite positive I know more than most people. Why am I so sure of this? Because I read. I watch television. And I mean more than The Cartoon Network and Comedy Central – though I like both of those. I travel. I go to movies. And best of all, I hang around smart people. That is about as important as anything you can do. Smart people have better conversations than stupid people. They know things. And they will share the things they know with you if you will just ask them. Smart people talk about things instead of people. That is one way you know you are talking to a smart person. So find yourself a smart person to hang around. Beware however, you might think they are a know-it-all.

Life is not about logic and reason and having a balanced checkbook. To think about and analyze life too much takes away the passion. Life is to be felt and lived. To the fullest. In every way. With everyone. All of the time.

So what if your checkbook won't balance and your world doesn't make sense? Have you seen a beautiful sunset today, or tumbled on the floor with your kids, or listened to a beautiful piece of music? Told someone how much you loved them? Have you let your soul soar and thanked your higher power for the blessing of being alive?

Logic and reason are highly overrated in my opinion. Let my right-brain rule my days...my passion, creativity, and emotions guide me into far more pleasurable places than my left-brain.

Lineage. So your daddy had money. I'm not impressed. So your grandfather was a big shot. I don't care. Who are *you*? What have *you* done?

My grandfather was a carney. Really – had a monkey and a bear and a pony ride and traveled with the carnival. My dad worked at Sears for forty-seven years. Impressed? Me neither. The point is that it doesn't matter. None of it does.

Who your parents were or weren't doesn't matter. Rich, intelligent parents can still have idiot kids who end up broke and stupid. Parents of modest means or no means at all can still have kids who do really well and end up rich.

You make of your life what you choose to make of your life. Period. That's good news for most kids, isn't it?

I hate the whole doctor experience. Not the actual "stuff" they do to you – that doesn't bother me at all. You can give me a root canal, a prostate exam, and Lasik surgery all at the same time and I really wouldn't care. But I hate filling out the paperwork and all of that stuff. And I hate to wait. I am a busy guy and I don't have time for that. Besides, I thought the very meaning of the word appointment pretty much meant that we *both* agreed to show up on time. Why do they get the right to be late and I don't? Why is it okay for them to saunter in forty-five minutes after the agreed time and act like nothing in the world is wrong?

If I don't show up to do my work on time I don't get paid. They shouldn't either.

"But they are doctors!"

So?

They have a specialty. Big deal. So do barbers and plumbers.

I like to sit on my patio as the sun goes down with my dog on my lap, a scotch by my side, a cigar in my hand, a little Willie Nelson in the background, talking to my wife. The other day I went to my humidor to get a cigar and since I didn't have my glasses on, I couldn't see the label on the cigar I pulled out. That was no big deal as I like all of my selections and I was really selecting by size more than brand. As Rose Mary and I sat and talked and watched the sun go down, I realized that the cigar I was smoking was truly spectacular. I asked Rose Mary to read the label to me so I would know what kind it was. She told me it was an Arturo Fuente Opus X. Well damn! I *guess* it was a good cigar! Cigar smokers know that the Opus X is *the* top of the heap: hard to find and very expensive. I had rat holed a few in my humidor of about one thousand smokes and was saving them for a special occasion. And now I found myself smoking one of my best cigars *just* to sit on the patio to watch the sun go down. I was disappointed that I had wasted a great cigar.

Then it hit me how stupid I was being. I should turn the moment into a celebration to match the cigar. I realized I wasn't wasting the cigar, I was wasting the experience. So I went back in the house, got a glass of Johnny Walker Blue, my best scotch, and came back out to make my normally ordinary time a time of real celebration.

I learned a good lesson. Don't wait for special occasions to enjoy your stuff. Use and enjoy your stuff to make normal occasions special. Now when I watch the sun go down, I smoke my finest and drink my best. Funny how much more I enjoy the time, the conversation, my wife, and even my dog. And realistically, that might be the last sunset I ever get to watch or the last great conversation I ever get to have with my best friend. I had better make the most of it!

Put on your best clothes and wear them to a "casual" dining experience. Put the good china on the table just to have breakfast with the family. Don't save that bottle of great champagne for a celebration. Instead break it out and toast a good day at work – or better yet, a bad day at work. Do whatever you can to turn normal occasions into special celebrations.

Contrary to popular belief,
there are stupid questions.

As seen on a T-shirt.
(Wish it were one of mine.)

One day I was walking through the parking lot of my grocery store heading toward the front door when I saw a guy who was obviously not handicapped getting out of his car he had just parked in the handicapped parking space. I yelled at him to get his attention and told him he needed to move his car since he wasn't handicapped. He asked how I knew he wasn't. I told him I didn't know ugly was an official handicap. He turned red, started to sweat and looked as if he were going to erupt when he finally blurted out, "Yeah and you're BALD!" I cracked up. I'm bald? Did he think this was news to me? I said to him, "That's the best you can come up with? I'm bald? Did you think I hadn't noticed that before?" At that point I just stood and continued to laugh in his face. He turned around and got back in his car and moved it. There is a very good chance someone really will beat the crap out of me someday. At least I want it to be for a good cause.

Don't park in a handicapped parking spot. If you do, then I believe the Universe will get even with you.

Common sense is no longer common.

Neither is common courtesy or
common knowledge.

larry winget

The Most Important
Key for Success in Business

Do what you say you are going to do, when
you say you are going to do it, in the way
you said you are going to do it.

Anything other than that is a lie.

213

You shouldn't have to work at friendship. Friendships should be easy. If you have to work to make it work, then it isn't really a friendship – it's just folks you hang around sometimes. Friends just accept you and let you be the way you are. They let you have your good days and bad days. They let you be an idiot and make an ass of yourself. They kick your butt when you need it. They will let you whine – but not for long. And you shouldn't have to work at that. It should just come naturally with a true friend.

Some people say marriages are like that. I disagree. My wife and I never work at our friendship. We work at our marriage every day. Our marriage is sometimes a wreck. Our friendship is always intact.

Better to have a good friend than a good spouse. If you can get them both in one, then you are way ahead. That doesn't always happen though.

Get a good friend and relax. Get a spouse and go to work.

"I wouldn't do that for love or money!"

Heard that?

Said that?

It's a lie. You would do anything for love or money. We all would. That's about all anybody really wants out of life: love and money.

Everything has a price. Nothing is free. No matter what it is in life you choose, it comes with a price tag attached.

Want to be fit, trim and healthy? The price is decreased calories and increased exercise.

Rich? You either have to work harder, longer, or smarter.

Successful? You have to do what the successful do. Read. Work. Believe. Dream. Have Goals. Take action.

Happy? The price is giving up everything that makes you unhappy.

larry winget

What you if don't want anything? That comes at a price too. The price usually is poverty, sickness, boredom, apathy, bad relationships and on and on.

The reality of life is you will pay a price one way or the other. One price gives you exactly what you want. The other gives you exactly what you don't want. Either way though, you have paid the price.

The good news is that the life you want comes cheaper than the life you don't want. The life you don't want makes you miserable, unhealthy and broke. To me, that is too big a price to pay. It's cheaper to be happy, rich and healthy. But you get to choose.

Shut Up Stop Whining And Get A Life.

My mantra. My theme. My slogan. What I say. What I sell. What people buy. Copyrighted. Trademarked. Mine. All mine.

So what does it mean?

Shut up. My Dad used to say most people are broadcasting when they ought to be tuned in. He meant they were so busy talking they couldn't hear what was being said. Good advice then and it still is. Most people need to shut up and listen. The Universe is sending us signals every day that most people never hear just because they are making so much noise. Smart people are talking to you. Great books are telling you exactly what to do. The Universe is screaming at you to pay attention. Shut up and listen.

Stop whining. No one wants to hear it anyway. It doesn't help the situation and it doesn't help you. Instead, take responsibility and get on with it. The mess you are in is your own fault. Your bad thinking and bad actions created your mess. And it is new thinking and new actions that will get you out of your mess. Abraham Lincoln said, "Don't complain and don't explain." Good idea.

Get a life. Get the life you want. You can create it whenever you choose to. It can be everything you ever dreamed of and wanted it to be. So do it. Now. No excuses. Just do what it takes to make it happen. Get the life you want. It is available whenever you choose to take it.

And you thought Shut Up Stop Whining And Get A Life was just a rant. It's not. It is a #1 National Bestseller. If you don't have it, buy it today!

Black & White

A_s I read all the stuff that I have written already for this book it seems like a good bit of it has to do with religion, sex and stupidity. I'm not sure why that is though I imagine it is because those are the most prevalent areas of our society. Stupidity reigns supreme. And sex sells everything and it is still society's biggest taboo and repressed area of expression. And then there is religion. Well, more harm has been done in the name of religion that I can even begin to cover. Don't argue with me on that one – I will win.

I think it is because we don't address these things head on. And we totally misunderstand all three.

Stupidity. We allow it. We tolerate it. We even condone it. It is our own fault. If we faced it head on we could fix a good portion of it. But we just don't. We have to attack stupidity by funding education and paying good teachers the way they should be paid and by clamping down on bad teachers and school systems that turn out stupid kids because they are too lazy to educate them. We have to make people accountable for their actions. Ignorance of the law is no excuse. You do the crime, you do the time. Stupidity is no excuse either. There are consequences and we should enforce them through our laws, our schools and the way we run our businesses. Which means that stupidity is *not* a legal defense.

Sex. We should educate kids about it. We should stop talking so much about what is morally right and start talking about what is healthy and responsible. We should let people know that sex is fun and a good thing to be enjoyed by people who love each other. And we should stop being so judgmental about what kind of sex is okay and what is not. If two legal adults want to do it and do it out of love and it isn't hurting you personally, then it is none of your business.

Religion. Religion has become less about love and more about money and politics and media exposure. Churches are scaring people away instead of just loving them.

Spirituality is more important than religious institutions. Love is more important than chastisement. Feeding hungry people is more important than preaching to them. (People can't listen when their stomachs are growling.) And acceptance is more important than judgment.

Churches should *en*courage (put the courage into) instead of *dis*courage (take the courage out of) people. Love can fix the world. Religion fills it with guilt and fear.

There. I've said it. I have explained myself. Deal with it.

People fight to get a parking place right in front of the exercise club then go inside and get on the treadmill.

Laws are not stupid. People are.
Policies are not stupid. People are.
Ideas are not stupid. People are.
Companies are not stupid. People are.
The government is not stupid. People are.

See a trend here?

Laws, policies and ideas don't just happen on their own. People created them. People agreed to put up with the laws and policies. (And they did agree otherwise they would have protested until they were changed.)

Companies are made up of people and everything about that company is a reflection of the people who own it, run it and work there.

Governments are made up of people. People elected by other people. Not always by the majority of people as we have proved right here in our own country, but still by people. And people just accept what the politicians do. Otherwise they would vote them out at the next election. Of course that would mean they would actually have to get out and vote.

So next time you say something is stupid, look behind the something at the people who are responsible. And look to yourself for putting up with it.

If you think a company is stupid, don't shop there or do business with them. If you continue to do business with a company you think is stupid, then you are the stupid one.

If you think a politician is stupid, vote against him or her. Get behind a candidate you do agree with.

If you think a law is stupid, then write your city council or go to a meeting or contact your Representative or Senator.

Do something. Speak up. Don't put up with stupidity. If you do, then you are just as guilty and just as stupid.

"Stupid is as stupid does."

Forrest Gump

I love to shop. I know that's an odd thing for most heterosexual guys, but I do. I have a black belt in shopping.

I like clothes. I like stuff. I like spending money. I like women's clothes too. (And I don't mean for me.) I just like fashion. And I like beautiful women in beautiful clothes. Is it any wonder one of my sons went into fashion design?

When my wife and I go shopping I love going through all of the racks of stuff and gathering up different outfits for her to try on. Believe me, she is tired long before I am. I am the husband who always says, "Buy it, buy it! If you buy it then I'll take you somewhere amazing to wear it." It usually works.

And shoes. I love shoes. Men's and women's. I have about a hundred pairs myself. If I didn't speak and write for a living, I would own a shoe store. No, it's not a fetish. I just like them, okay?

I like malls. Especially during football season. I don't like football. But I love to shop. If you like to shop then go to the mall on a Sunday afternoon during football season. It is practically empty – except for women. (Guys, that's a good thing.)

If you like to people-watch, the mall is a great place. If you are a guy, the mall is also full of hotties. One of my sons hates to shop, but he sure likes the girls at the mall. Plus there are plenty of good restaurants and bars if you get tired of shopping.

So what is the point of this thing? Beats me. Wait, I know. This is a dating tip. Women like men who know about clothes and who like to shop. There you go, I knew there had to be a point to this.

See you at the mall.

Willpower. Totally over-rated.

I don't have much. I admit it. I have a problem saying no to things I enjoy.

For instance: my wife buys things we both love to eat. Things that are not good for us and that we don't really want to eat. She does that so she can have them there in the cabinets and then deny herself those things through the use of her willpower. This makes her feel good. The problem is, I don't have any willpower. If it is there, I will eat it. And denial is just not my style. Indulgence is my style.

Lack of opportunity works for me. If you give me the opportunity, I'll take it. Regarding any thing at any time in any situation. I capitalize on all opportunities. So the only thing I can do is limit my opportunities to do the things I shouldn't do.

I don't think I am that unique in this. I don't think many people have much willpower. At least not enough to really be able to count on it in times of real need. The best thing they can do is just not put themselves in a position where they can say yes to doing the wrong thing.

Limit your options. That's the key.

Some religions teach that suicide is a sin.

Why is it that taking a gun, shooting yourself and ending your life in a split second is a sin and overeating and smoking and killing yourself over thirty years isn't? The end result is the same isn't it? You did it to yourself didn't you?

It must not be the killing that is sinful, it must just be the timing of it. Right?

I want to ask those huge gluttonous pious preachers on TV that question.

Y ou know those little kids in the mall and in restaurants that are just so bad? So ill-behaved you just want to jerk them up yourself and take control of the situation? Those little kids drive me crazy. But what I have to remind myself is that little kids are not bad. There are no bad little kids, there are only bad parents. It is not the little kid's fault he is running around screaming through the restaurant. It is the parents' fault. The little kid does not need a talking to, the mama and daddy do. Little kids behave the way they are allowed to behave. They push the limits. They are supposed to. It is part of growing up. It is the responsibility of the parents to set limits and boundaries the child can live within. Then discipline accordingly when they don't.

A lack of discipline is a lack of love in my opinion. Parents, love your kids enough to discipline them. I am not saying spank them or stand them in a corner or give them time out. That is your business. But be consistent and make the punishment fit the crime. And do it in private. Don't scream and smack your kids in front of the rest of the world. It is embarrassing to the kid and a bother to those who have to witness it.

When I was growing up, my dad would often say "When we get home you are going to get a whipping." (My dad gave whippings, with a belt, hard. Not abusive and not often. But when I got one, I didn't soon forget it.) And it didn't matter whether he told me that on the first day of a two week vacation, when we got home, even though not one more word had been said about it for two weeks, I got my whipping. My dad taught me a lot. One of the things was that his word was golden. A promise is a promise no matter what the promise is about.

Though I didn't appreciate that much when being promised a whipping, I appreciate it now.

People want to change the world. Here is a news flash: the world doesn't want to be changed.

Besides, even if it did, you couldn't do it.

Politicians want to change the world. So do preachers. And my business, the business of professional speaking, exists simply because a group of people want to change the world too.

At one point in my life and career, even I wanted to change the world. Not any more. It is about all I can do to change myself. How do you motivate others when you can barely haul your tired butt out of bed in the morning? I can't. So I gave it up. I can only work on me. The world is on its own.

However, that is the key. Change yourself. That is how the world gets changed. Individuals taking individual responsibility for their thoughts and actions.

As Shakespeare said, "Therein lies the rub."

It is much easier to make plans to change the world than it is to change yourself.

Here is my message:

Clean up your own back yard. Change by example. Live the way you want others to live. Don't worry so much about how others live. Just be the way you want others to be and hope they pay attention.

Then write a few books, record some tapes and videos and give a hundred or so speeches a year and hope people give you some money to do it.

Concerts must be confusing. They aren't to me and they probably aren't to you, but they seem to be to a good number of people.

Just a few minutes ago I got back from a Lyle Lovett concert. The ticket clearly said Lyle Lovett And His Large Band. It did not say Lyle Lovett and the large man in Section 5, Row 27, Seat 6. The ticket clearly said concert; it did not say sing-a-long.

When I go to a concert I pay to hear the artist perform. Don't you? I do not want to hear *anyone* else singing. I want everyone to have a great time and enjoy the concert and leave happy. But that does not mean you have the right to sing and stand in your chair and

dance in front of me so I can neither see nor
hear the guy I paid to see.

Another thing. The ticket clearly states the
time the concert begins. Tonight it said
7:30 p.m. It did not say 7:40 or 7:55. It
was printed in pretty big letters: 7:30. That
means you should be in your seat at 7:30
waiting in anticipation for the first note to be
played. It doesn't mean you should be in line
getting your beer at 7:30 so you can stumble
across me and dribble on me getting to your
seat after the concert has started.

And here is the most important thing I
learned tonight at the Lyle Lovett concert:

I need back-up singers.

Exercise. I hate it. Really, I just hate it. I do it but I don't like it at all.

Some people say they like it. I don't understand those people.

I like chocolate. I understand people who like chocolate.

Actually chocolate is the reason I exercise. If I didn't exercise I would be shaped like an M&M.

So while I don't like it, I am still willing to do it. I do it so I can have the option of a dark chocolate truffle every once in a while – or a bag of M&M's.

That's pretty much the case with everything in life. You have to do what it takes in order to get what you want. Enjoyment always comes at a price.

Even M&M's.

At the end of the day what really matters? A guy asked me that yesterday during an interview. It was the best question I have ever been asked in an interview. Know what I answered? Of course you don't, so let me tell you: Not much. Really, not much matters. At the end of the day if you smiled more than you frowned, laughed more than cried, told your family and friends that you loved them and had a pretty good time doing what you do for a living, then it was a good day. Go to bed and say thanks. That's about it.

Larry Winget

The World's Only Irritational Speaker®
and
The Pitbull of Personal Development®

Larry Winget is a philosopher of success who just happens to be hilarious. He teaches universal principles that will work for anyone, in any business, at any time, and does it by telling funny stories. He believes that most of us have complicated life and business way too much, take it way too seriously and that we need to lighten up, take responsibility, be more flexible, stay positive and keep it in perspective. He believes that success and prosperity come from serving others. He teaches that business improves when the people in the business improve and that everything in life gets better when we get better and nothing gets better until we get better.